Inspirations for DANCE & MOVE

Published by Scholastic Ltd,
Villiers House,
Clarendon Avenue,
Leamington Spa,
Warwickshire CV32 5PR

© 1994 Scholastic Ltd.
Revised edition 1996

Written by Judy Evans and
Hazel Powell
Edited by Jo Saxelby-Jennings
Sub-edited by Catherine Baker
Revised edition edited by Joanne Boden
Designed by Micky Pledge
Series designed by Juanita Puddifoot
Illustrated by Francis Scappaticci
(Maggie Mundy Agency)
Cover artwork by Julie Anderson
(Pennant Agency)
Attainment target charts prepared by
Gill Friel (Scotland) and Ray Gilbert
and Jennifer Boyd of the South-
Eastern Education and Library Board
(NI)

Designed using Aldus Pagemaker
Processed by Studio Photoset, Leicester
Artwork by Steve Williams &
Associates, Leicester
Printed in Great Britain by
Ebenezer Baylis & Son, Worcester

**British Library Cataloguing in
Publication Data**
A catalogue record for this book is
available from the British Library.

ISBN 0-590-53514-5 2nd revised edition
(ISBN 0-590-53089-5 1st edition)

Acknowledgements

The publishers gratefully
acknowledge permission to
reproduce the following
copyright material.

'The Autumn leaves have fallen
down' from *This Little Puffin*
edited by Elizabeth Matterson,
copyright © 1969. Published in
Puffin Books.
'Caterpillars only crawl' by
Peter Charlton and Sue
Charlton © 1972 Reproduced
by permission of Keith Prowse
Music Publishing Company
Limited, London WC2H 0EA.
© James Reeves for 'Fireworks'
from *The Wandering Moon and
Other Poems* (Puffin Books) by
James Reeves. Reprinted by
permission of the James
Reeves Estate.
'Jack Frost' by Cecily E. Pike
reproduced by kind
permission of National
Christian Education Council.
Extracts from *Jonathan
Livingston Seagull: A story*
reproduced by kind
permission of Turnstone Press,
an imprint of HarperCollins
Publishers Limited.
'The litter bug' from *Grizzly
Tales for Gruesome Kids*
by J. Rix © 1990, reproduced
by kind permission of André
Deutsch Children's Books.

Every effort has been made to
trace copyright holders. The
publishers apologise for any
inadvertent omissions.

CONTENTS

Dance and movement

Dance is fun. Everyone can dance, regardless of their age, ability, sex or cultural background. Young children dance naturally, responding to rhythm, music and mood. Intrinsic satisfaction, enjoyment and pleasure can be gained from the sensation of moving for its own sake. Movement comes before words as a means of expression, exploration and communication. It is the child's first language. He will clap his hands and jump for joy or stamp his feet with annoyance and frustration.

Movement that has rhythm and phrasing, together with the specific intention of giving expression to particular ideas, is 'dance'. Dance explores the expressive potential of movement and in dance progression is made from natural movement to increased technical movement skills.

Dance can make a distinctive contribution to the education of all children, in that it uses the most fundamental mode of human expression – movement. Through the use of non-verbal communication children are able to participate in a way that differs from any other area of learning. Some children can express themselves far better through dance than through the written or spoken word.

There is, however, a very important relationship between language development and movement. The choice of words when introducing an activity or an idea stimulates the children's imaginations which in turn influences their movement responses.

Dance can help a child to understand the expressive nature of his actions. He can build up a movement vocabulary. He can explore the dynamic qualities of movement and the spatial patterns that can be created when working alone, with a partner or in a small or large group.

The National Curriculum Physical Education Working Group Interim Report (1991) offered the following definition of dance:
'Dance is a distinct art form, with its own history, body of knowledge, aesthetic values, cultural contexts and artistic products. It offers a variety of learning opportunities and enables participants to enjoy physical experiences as well as develop intellectual sensibilities. Pupils can understand themselves and others by learning in and through dance. Dance also provides particular opportunities for cross-curricular work.'

Dance is a broad umbrella term that incorporates a wide range of different styles and forms.

It is outlined in *Physical Education for Ages 5 to 16* (DES, 1991) that: 'Dance in its broad cultural context includes three interrelated categories:
• popular culture/art: dance of the time, for example, Bhangra, Jazz, Ballroom, Tap, Street Dancing, Ballet, Contemporary, South Asian forms, African People's Dance, New Dance;
• traditional/folk: dances from different countries, for example, Morris, Clog, some Asian forms, some African People's Dance; and
• historical: dances of the past, for example, *Farandole, Charleston, Minuet, Tango, Lindy Hop.*'

In the primary school, the dance curriculum will be concerned mainly with creative dance (which is the focus of this book). In addition, this should be supported by the inclusion of traditional dance, folk dance and historical dance where appropriate. Through dance, children may learn more about their own cultural heritage, as well as learning dances from other times and places. This will provide them with a basis for understanding the different cultural values and traditions attached to dance. Such a curriculum will give access to the rich diversity of dance and provide the foundation for dance in its broad cultural context.

Dance as an art form

Dance is an art form; it is a performing art in its own right with its own separate history, body of knowledge (language) and understanding. The distinctiveness of dance comes from the intention and ability to make symbolic movements which express and communicate meaning. This is what distinguishes dance from other physical activities such as gymnastics. Dance is concerned with physical skills and the physical potential of the body; movements can be taught in a particular way and then explored and developed, but it is the *intention* behind the movement which is emphasised rather than just for exercise or functional movement.

Dance shows characteristics in common with the other arts and a common language can be established for describing elements which are found across the arts, such as 'form', 'space', 'rhythm', and 'line'. Dance is unique among the arts: '... unless filmed it is inseparable from the fleeting movement. In this it differs from the "frozen" arts of painting and literature.' (D. Best, cited in P.J. Arnold, 1979, *Meaning in Movement, Sport and Physical Education*, Heinemann Educational Books).

Dance as an art model develops in children an appreciation of dance as an artistic and aesthetic activity. Dance contributes to a child's artistic and aesthetic education because it provides an opportunity for her to engage in the processes of exploring, creating, selecting, refining, performing and critically appraising her own work and that of others, including professional artists.

In the primary school curriculum, dance makes a valuable contribution as an art form while also contributing to a balanced physical education programme and enhancing cross-curricular learning. Children are provided with an opportunity to learn in and through dance.

 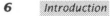

Dance in the National Curriculum

In the Physical Education National Curriculum for England and Wales, dance is identified as one of the areas of activity into which the curriculum is divided. In each year of Key Stage 1 all pupils should be taught three areas of activity; Games, Gymnastic activities and Dance. At Key Stage 2 pupils should be taught Games, Dance, Swimming and Gymnastic Activities, Athletic Activities, Outdoor /Adventurous Activities. Each area of activity offers a different kind of learning experience and reflects different characteristics: 'Dance forms ... focus on the body and ... emphasise the artistic and expressive aspects of movement ...' (DES, *Physical Education for Ages 5 to 16*, 1991).

Dance is also acknowledged as a core physical activity in the Scottish and Northern Irish guidelines.

As physical education is a foundation subject in England and Wales, it is the *entitlement* of all children to have access to dance and is one of the major areas of experience in the primary school.

The *statutory* requirements for physical education in England and Wales include:
• *one attainment target*, which involves the children in the continuous process of planning, performing and evaluating;
• *end of key stage descriptions* for each key stage, which express the broad expectations of the knowledge, skills and understanding the children should be able to demonstrate by the end of each key stage;
• *programmes of study*, which consist of common and general requirements, general and activity-specific programmes of study, providing at each key stage a framework for a broad and balanced dance curriculum.

The order for physical education is based on the continuous process of planning, performing and evaluating. In dance, we use the same processes but adopt the terminology of *composing,*

performing and *appreciating;* where *composing* involves planning and *appreciating* involves evaluation:
• Composing provides opportunities for young children to plan and make their own dances.
• Performing is an important aspect as dance is a 'performing art'. Children are involved in performing when creating their dances and should be encouraged to see their performance in terms of both personal attainment and presentation for an audience. The audience may be the teacher, a partner, another group, the whole class, the whole school (as at an assembly) or from beyond the immediate school community (as at an Open Day).
• Appreciation encourages children to observe and evaluate dance and comment appropriately. Through watching their peers and professional artists they learn to respond to dance and to make discerning judgements. This critical appraisal is the beginnings of aesthetic appreciation.

Dance and cross-curricular links

Dance is a mode of learning in its own right and can be a vehicle for the promotion of learning in other areas across the curriculum. For example, the strong link between language development and movement has already been mentioned. Movement vocabulary can extend language by encouraging children to think creatively. Different ways of jumping might include 'bouncing', 'leaping', 'bounding', 'tossing', 'flying', 'exploring', 'springing', 'bursting', and so on (see 'Stimuli for dance – Action words' in Chapter 1, page 24.) Dance can also help children grasp concepts such as going 'over', 'under', 'in', 'out', 'around' and 'through' to enable them to develop a greater understanding of language. To help their understanding of mathematical concepts, children can step out the patterns of circles, squares and triangles on the floor. In this way, they will gain more of a feel for and an understanding of shape than they would get by looking at a flat shape on a piece of paper. Understanding of number can be enhanced through the use of counts in warming-up, moving to phrases of eight or four counts and so on in various combinations. Rhythmic patterns should be remembered and repeated. Line, shape and symmetry can all be explored through dance and linked to mathematics and art. Dance has obvious links with developing knowledge and understanding about the body and how it moves and works. The importance of warm-up and exercise to maintain a healthy heart and an enhanced understanding of stamina, mobility, flexibility, strength and coordination makes links with both science and other areas of physical education. The physical aspects of movement – energy, time and space – can help understanding of 'forces'.

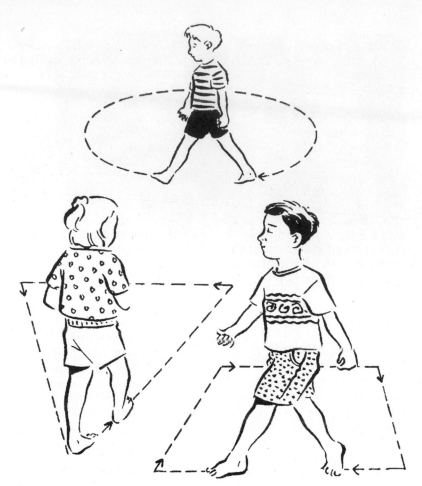

Dance also provides opportunities for children to take part and perform individually, as well as being part of a group. Initiative is encouraged and self-confidence developed as the children learn more about themselves and develop a sensitivity and a greater awareness of others. The ability to work independently and to both lead and cooperate with others are essential elements of dance education and provide opportunities for success which will not only enhance self-esteem but also contribute to personal and social development. Communication skills are developed through movement and ideas and values can be explored. A creative activity such as dance can also enhance creativity in many other curricular areas such as art, drama, or music. Dance can be seen as contributing to several areas of the curriculum. It can also be a vehicle for drawing together different areas of the curriculum and act as a stimulus to work being carried out in these other areas.

Implementing dance in school

In order to plan and implement dance effectively in the National Curriculum, schools need to develop a systematic approach to curriculum planning. The National Curriculum Council states: 'Our approach is therefore to encourage schools to take an objective look at their existing curriculum organisation, to build on strengths, and to modify their plans where necessary.' (*Planning the National Curriculum at Key Stage 2*, 1993).

To aid the planning process a number of questions should be considered.
• Do the pupils have access to a broad and balanced programme in physical education?

At Key Stage 1 all children should be taught three areas of activity as specified in the National Curriculum and, in addition, swimming if they choose to do so. While at Key Stage 2 they should have access to all six areas of the curriculum with an emphasis on gymnastics, dance and games.
• Does your school have a policy statement for dance?

Each school should have its own policy statement for physical education which should include a statement on dance, reasons for its inclusion and how dance should be implemented through the curriculum. The policy statement should link into the whole school philosophy and policy.

• Does your school have a clear set of aims for dance?

The aims for dance should reflect and meet the requirements of the National Curriculum, and should encourage the children to demonstrate knowledge, skills and understanding of the processes of composing, performing and appreciating. 'Physical Education educates young people in and through the use and knowledge of the body and its movement. ...[It] aims to develop physical competence so that pupils are able to move efficiently, effectively and safely and understand what they are doing. It is essentially a way of learning through action, awareness and observation.' (DES, *Physical Education for Ages 5 to 16,* 1991).
• Has your school developed schemes of work for dance?

A scheme of work for dance should consider overall, long-term planning using the Common and General Requirements, the Programmes of Study for Dance and End of Key Stage Descriptions as a basis and may consist of several units of

work. We recommend that you develop one scheme of work across Key Stage 1 and two schemes of work across Key Stage 2. Each scheme of work should have a rationale with clear aims and learning objectives and should reflect the school policy statement, allocate an appropriate amount of time to follow the programmes of study, promote continuity and progression, differentiation, teaching and learning styles, assessment, recording and reporting.
• Has your school developed units of work in dance?

The individual units of work will vary in length depending on the idea or topic in which the class are involved. For example, a unit of work for infants may last three weeks, but with juniors a unit of work may last five or perhaps seven weeks, depending on the nature of the work. Planning units of work should include and link into the Common and General requirements, Programmes of Study for Dance and End of Key Stage Descriptions. Examples of units of work for dance are given in the *Non-statutory Guidelines* (*Physical Education*) (NCC, June 1992).
• Has each teacher developed detailed lesson plans for dance?

Lessons should be planned by the individual teacher using the schemes and units of work as a basis, which will enable links to be made with other areas of the curriculum.
• Does your school have adequate resources for implementing dance?

To implement dance in the National Curriculum careful consideration needs to be made in the provision of adequate resources and equipment.

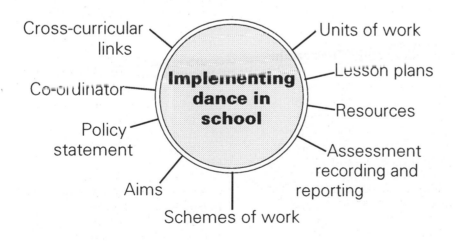

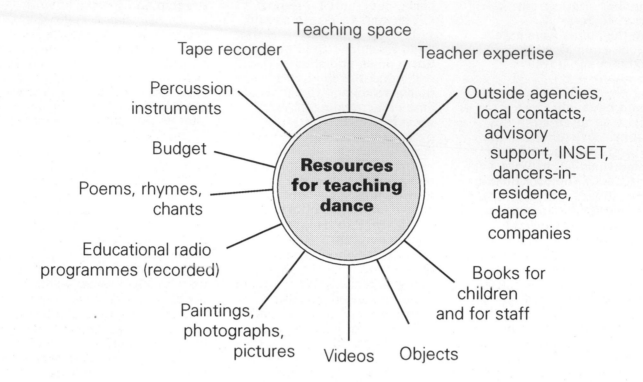

Resyources for teaching dance:
- Teaching space
- Tape recorder
- Teacher expertise
- Percussion instruments
- Outside agencies, local contacts, advisory support, INSET, dancers-in-residence, dance companies
- Budget
- Poems, rhymes, chants
- Educational radio programmes (recorded)
- Books for children and for staff
- Paintings, photographs, pictures
- Videos
- Objects

However, the most important resources for dance are the commitment, enthusiasm and expertise of the teacher. You do not need to be a professionally trained dancer to teach creative dance, but you do need to be committed and enthusiastic. With adequate facilities (such as a large, clear space and a tape recorder), resources can be built up with careful planning and some financial allowance. For example, a library of music recordings, videos and books for use by the children and teacher and a range of percussion instruments and appropriate stimuli (see page 23, 'Stimuli for dance') should be collected. Resources and advice may also be forthcoming through links with outside agencies such as the local advisory support and

dance companies.
• Can links be made with other areas of the curriculum?

When using a topic or thematic approach, rigorous planning and preparation need to be considered. The model we use in this book is only one possible way of working but has been used successfully by many teachers. When planning a topic, it is essential to have clearly identified aims. Select two or three subjects with common elements to enable you to study the topic in depth and ensure that a balance of time is devoted to each subject. It is essential to consider the statements of attainment, end of key stage statements and programmes of study in the subject planning. Once the topic has been planned for each subject, the curriculum can then be strengthened by making links

with other subject areas. For example work in one subject area may be the stimulus for work in another, a piece of creative writing produced in English may be the stimulus for a dance lesson, or a piece of music might be composed and the structure and rhythm used to develop a dance. Try to avoid contrived links, but look at linking subjects in a way which will make the curriculum relevant and workable.
• Have you developed assessment, recording and reporting?

Children are to be assessed in physical education at the end of each key stage. Assessment of the children's work should be a continuous process to inform pupils, teachers and parents about the progress of each individual child. Further information

about assessment is given in Chapter 3, 'Assessment in dance', on page 39.
• Who is responsible for initiating and maintaining dance in your school?

It is essential that all schools have a coordinator for physical education or a member of staff with responsibility for this area of the curriculum in order to implement the National Curriculum. The coordinator's responsibilities should include areas such as: writing a policy statement; planning and developing schemes and units of work in consultation with all members of staff; ensuring there is adequate provision of resources and equipment; and helping, supporting and advising staff in developing dance. Developing the dance curriculum is an ongoing process of planning, implementing, reviewing, evaluating and modifying.

Equal opportunities in dance

'All pupils should receive a broad and balanced programme of physical education which is differentiated to meet their needs and which coincides with their interests. All children should be allowed access to and given confidence in the different activities involved, regardless of their ability, sex, or cultural/ethnic background.' (DES, *Physical Education for Ages 5 to 16*, 1991).

All children should be given the opportunity to learn in and through dance at each stage of their education. The National Curriculum Council has identified equal opportunities as a cross-curricular dimension which should permeate all subjects. Equal opportunities should be a part of the whole school policy and should show commitment and sensitivity through good and effective teaching and be actively promoted throughout education.

'Working towards equality of opportunity requires that teachers should treat all children as individuals with their own abilities, difficulties and attitudes.' (DES, *Physical Education for Ages 5 to 16*, 1991).

In dance education, this means *all* children, regardless of their ability, sex or cultural or ethnic background, should have equal access and opportunity to dance and it is the responsibility of all teachers to ensure that equal access and opportunity is provided. The Arts Council suggests in *Dance in Schools* (1993) that 'the dance programme should be based on the following principles:
• *entitlement* – all children are entitled to dance education as part of the broad and balanced physical education programme of the National Curriculum.
• *accessibility* – to ensure all pupils are provided with access to dance requires positive action to challenge prejudice and stereotyping, a programme of work that is inclusive of all pupils and is relevant, challenging and achievable.
• *integration* – through working together young people of different abilities, cultures and backgrounds are more able to appreciate and value the contributions and achievements of their peers.
• *integrity* – all activities should be meaningful and contain educational purpose.'

Gender issues

In the primary school, it is important that dance is taught as a mixed-sex activity and that girls and boys are given the opportunity to dance together. It should not be offered as an activity for girls while the boys play football, for example. Dance is often seen as a feminine activity and inappropriate for boys. You must look sensitively at the ways in which dance is taught to boys and girls, and encourage a variety of groupings within the dance programme, to offer a balance, so that sometimes boys and girls choreograph and perform a dance together, sometimes girls dance together and sometimes boys dance together. Encourage them also to evaluate and appreciate each other's work. It is also essential that both male and female teachers are seen to teach dance in order to promote positive role models. This can also be achieved by inviting dance companies into school or by taking the children to the theatre to see dance performances where they have the opportunity to watch male and female dancers perform together.

Special needs

'Dance has a particular contribution to make to pupils with special educational needs. It provides them with an alternative language and route for learning about themselves, others and the world around them.' (DES, *Physical Education for Ages 5 to 16*, 1991).

Children with special educational needs will require additional consideration in order to participate in dance, whether they are in special schools or integrated into mainstream education. Dance, by definition, involves movement and will have a unique effect on the kind of programme offered to the young child with learning difficulties. However, the programmes of study for dance can be made accessible to all pupils with special educational needs with very little modification. You will need to plan individual movement programmes to suit particular challenges. For example, how can the teacher modify the dance lesson for the young child with hearing problems who may not be able to hear the music or the child in the wheelchair who wants to be able to participate in a country dancing lesson with able-bodied children? A young child with partial hearing may not be able to hear music to accompany dance, but he may respond to the vibrations of a drum or a variety of other stimuli such as poetry, pictures or props. The child in a wheelchair can choreograph and perform a country dance with able-bodied children using patterns and pathways as a starting point instead of a variety of steps. When planning a dance programme for children with special needs it is important to recognise the demands of the different groups; sensory impairments, movement problems, moderate to profound and multiple learning difficulties, medical conditions, emotional and behavioural disorders, and the gifted child. All these children should have the opportunity to move and dance to build up their confidence and ability to move, to enable them to join in with their own peer group, be able to structure their ideas and feelings through movement and have a positive and enjoyable experience. For some children, performing a dance may come easily, but the planning and evaluating may be very difficult; for other children the performance may be difficult, but they may be able to compose and appreciate dances to a high standard. It is, therefore, very important that the dance programme is modified to enable these children to achieve and progress in the areas where they show strengths. Children who have difficulty in expressing themselves through language may be able to communicate their ideas through movement. Children communicate by using language to shape and convey thoughts and feelings and dance provides a medium in which the meaning of words can be reinforced and the development of language helped. This book shows the interaction between language and movement, and with every lesson there is a list of action words which relate to what the children can do, and where, how, and with whom they can move. For example, in Chapter 15, 'Stories' (page 147), in the lesson 'In the Wild Wood', the children are encouraged to relate to the words: 'creeping', 'chasing', 'searching', 'skipping', 'trembling' and so on. Children who have difficulty in grasping the concepts of words such as 'over', 'under', 'around' and 'through' will gain a greater understanding by experiencing going through the space, around a partner, and under or over a shape made by someone else in the class. Those children with movement difficulties can be encouraged through dance to control their movements and be physically challenged. For example, a child with a walking frame could be encouraged to make up a dance phrase individually or with a partner using the frame as part of the dance, to support different parts of her body and to use as an extension of her body shape. A child in a wheelchair can perform all the actions and ideas a dance lesson in this book provides, using the chair to travel, turn, change direction and speed, and using the upper body to bend, stretch, twist and gesture. The only movement which may present him with a problem is the action of jumping and here he may be able to lift his body up out of his chair.

'It is important to concentrate on pupils' abilities and needs, not on their disabilities and handicaps. This emphasis aims to improve their movement skills and helps to change feelings of disaffection, under-achievement and low self-esteem.' (NCC, *Non-statutory Guidance [Physical Education]*, 1992).

Cultural diversity

'All dances have a cultural context. Dance can provide a focus for multicultural education, and dances from a range of cultures should be studied for their contribution to both dance and multicultural education.' (The Arts Council, *Dance in Schools*, 1993).

All teachers need to be aware of and sensitive to the cultural diversity of our schools and should address the issues of race and ethnic, cultural, social and religious heritage. Schools need to recognise the variety of cultural forms in dance. 'Through learning a range of dances and by using their place in religious festivals as a focus for multicultural education, pupils can recognise the richness and diversity of cultures other than their own...' (DES, *Physical Education for Ages 5 to 16*, 1991) and 'Pupils can share their traditional dances and they may bring into school a rich movement vocabulary and different understanding of dance...' (The Arts Council, *Dance in Schools*, 1993).

Problems may occur in dance lessons for some religious and cultural groups, but with consideration and negotiation all pupils should be able to participate fully. For example, some girls may need to be taught in single sex groups, avoid physical contact, wear appropriate clothing to retain modesty or avoid public performances. Special consideration should also be given to diet, hygiene and religious observances; for example, you should be aware of the limitations of children required to take exercise during fasting.

About this book

This book has been written as a resource for dance to support teachers working with children from the ages of five to eleven years. The content of the book considers and explains the language used in dance which is 'the body of knowledge' and shows a simple planning process for implementing dance as an integral part of the primary curriculum. The book includes the movement content of a dance programme showing continuity and progression, the process of planning and structuring a lesson using a range of stimuli, learning intentions and outcomes, assessment and evaluation and a simple method of recording. Understanding these elements will provide teachers with the knowledge and content of a dance programme and will enable them to plan their schemes, units of work and individual lesson plans across each key stage. Key Stage 1 spans two school years, but Key Stage 2 spans four school years. We have divided this second stage into two clear age groups, seven to nine years and nine to eleven years, to aid planning, progression and continuity.

The lesson examples have been designed using a topic-based approach, as we believe that this method is an effective way of incorporating dance into the curriculum while, at the same time, making it accessible to the non-specialist. A variety of topics have been selected that are used regularly in the primary curriculum. Each chapter is devoted to one specific topic and includes a topic web of dance ideas and examples of starter lessons which could be developed in subsequent sessions, together with stimuli and movement themes, appropriate for each of the three age groups: five to seven years, seven to nine years and nine to eleven years. Each example lesson contains ideas for an introduction, movement development and a dance idea, learning outcomes, and further suggestions for follow-up work in dance. The material provided in each example is more than enough for one lesson and may, in some cases, be used to develop the dance idea over a series of lessons. Photocopiable material is also provided to support the text and can be used to assist planning and pupil self-assessment and as evidence for teacher assessment.

CHAPTER 1

The language of dance

This chapter seeks to explain the body of knowledge in dance, which is the theory upon which the dance lessons in this book have been based. An analysis of movement content is included and clearly summarised as a photocopiable chart.

Progression in dance is also addressed, and suitable stimuli for dance and simple choreographic ideas are discussed to help you with structuring dance.

Movement content

Dance is movement in time and space. The interaction between intention, body action, dynamics, space, relationships, stimulus and accompaniment is the *content* of the dance. This content is then shaped and structured to give form to the dance.

In order to help the children to develop knowledge, skills and understanding in dance and to improve the quality and variety in their work it is important that the teacher has a clear understanding of the movement content first, as this is the starting point for teaching dance. The movement content can be analysed as follows so that there are four main areas to consider:

• Body actions – what is the body doing?
• Dynamics – how does the body move?
• Space – where does the body move?
• Relationships – with whom and with what can we dance?

Body actions

First, what actions can the body do? Initially, young children will be concerned with the actions that involve their whole bodies in stepping, travelling, jumping, turning, gesture and stillness. They will then discover that the body can also bend, stretch, twist, open, close, extend and contract and, as these actions are performed, the body will make the different shapes of wide, narrow, round or twisted. Shapes can also be made where the body is symmetrical, so that both the right and the left sides of the body are doing exactly the same. Conversely, the body can make asymmetrical shapes where the right and left sides do not match exactly.

A particular part of the body, such as the head, shoulders, elbows, hips, knees and so on can also be emphasised or isolated, so that part of the body only will be moving. Selected parts can move all at the same time, that is simultaneously, or they can move so that one body part follows on from the next in succession. For example, the whole arm (shoulder, elbow, wrist, hand) can be raised at the same time, or the shoulder could rise, followed by the elbow, then the wrist and finally the hand. In addition, one part of the body can be selected to lead or initiate a movement; for example, the leg may sweep around the body to take the body into a turning movement.

A suitable task for children at Key Stage 1 children would be to ask them to travel in a variety of ways such as walking, running, hopping, skipping and galloping. At Key Stage 2, the children would be able to travel, turn and jump, performing a more complex task by linking the movements together. Alternatively, at Key Stage 1 children would be able to perform individual body shapes while at Key Stage 2 they would be able to change from one body shape to a different body shape.

Dynamics

Second, the dynamics of how the body can move needs to be considered. For example, the movement can be performed so that it is very slow, or sustained over a period of time, or the movement can be very quick and sudden. Young children will need to experience the contrast of quick and slow to understand what 'quick' is and how it feels, compared to a slow, ongoing movement. Similarly, movements can be performed so that they are very strong and firm or, in contrast, very light. The movement may cut directly through the space; for example, the hand could start near the centre of the body and shoot straight upwards or, in contrast, the movement could take a very roundabout, or flexible, route. Movements

can be very controlled so that they can be stopped and started at will or they can be very much freer and more abandoned so that it is quite difficult to stop immediately.

At Key Stage 1, children would be able to perform a quick turn or a slow turn, a strong step or a light step. By Key Stage 2, they should be able to perform a more complex task, combining these elements, such as a quick, light jump or a strong, slow step.

Space

The third area to consider is where the body moves in the space. Movements may be on the spot, so that everyone has his or her own personal space to move in, or the children may be weaving around each other using the whole of the general space available.

Movements can also be performed at a variety of levels, so that the children are working near to the floor, for example, they could sink down to the ground; this would be moving at a low level. In contrast to this, reaching or jumping high into the air would be moving at a high level. In between would be the medium level.

When asked to move around the hall, the natural direction that the majority of children choose would be forwards. Their attention needs to be drawn to the fact that movements can be performed in other directions, such as backwards, sideways, upwards, downwards and diagonally.

As the body moves forwards the resulting action is said to be 'advancing', while moving backwards would be seen as 'retreating'. Similarly, moving upwards would be 'rising', while moving downwards would be 'sinking'. When moving sideways, if the right-hand side of the body is being used, then in taking the movement to the right the body would be said to be 'opening', but taking the right hand or foot to the left would result in the body performing a 'closing' action.

As the dance phrase is performed, an imaginary trace pattern could be followed. This can be both on the floor and in the air and the resulting pattern could be a straight line, curved, twisted or angular.

A suitable task for Key Stage 1 pupils, would be to ask them to include a change in level *or* a change of direction in their dance phrase. Asking the same children to include a change in level *and* direction would be a more complex task to set them and, therefore, would be better left until Key Stage 2.

Relationship

The final area to consider when composing dances, is that of the relationship, that is to say with whom or with what the children will be dancing. If the relationship is with you, the teacher, the children could be asked to creep towards you and then run away, or alternatively, they could move around you. You could reach up high and ask the children to do the same as you or you could ask them to do the opposite to you. These are all popular ways of asking particularly young children to move.

The children could be asked to work individually, but all at the same time, so that they are all busily working on their own movement phrases. In each of their selected phrases one part of the body, for example the elbow, may come close to or even contact another part of the body, such as the knee, so that their is a relationship between these two parts of the body.

Introducing another person, so that the children are working in pairs, creates many possibilities for dance. Both children could do exactly the same actions or they could do the opposite, so that, for example, as one partner reaches high the other partner sinks low. They might decide to start the dance apart and at a certain place in the dance come together so that they meet. A decision then needs to be made about whether they stay together or part again. One partner may become a leader so that the other person has to follow the movements or the pathway travelled. The pair may decide to work together, but one may act as a reflection of the other, like a mirror. Alternatively, one partner may decide to be still while the other partner travels around him and they could then change over roles. A situation may be created where one partner performs part of the dance phrase, while the other partner observes this and makes a response to it in movement. This is called 'question and answer'. Children, particularly at Key Stage 2, usually discover that working with a partner can be both interesting and enjoyable.

As more children work together the number of possible permutations and the variety in the way that they work and their formations increases enormously. Groups may be small, such as a trio, or may be larger including as many as seven children. The group shape may change throughout the dance, for example, from a circle to a cluster or a line. The children in the group can all move at the same time, so that they are in 'unison', or may move one after the other, which is called 'canon'.

A suitable task at Key Stage 1 would be to make up a step pattern and individually perform their dances towards and away from the teacher. By the end of Key Stage 1 the children should be able to perform their dance in pairs, meeting and parting. At Key Stage 2, they should be able to perform their step patterns together in a large group, meeting and parting and changing formation and the shapes of their groups.

Movement content

Body action – what the body can do	Dynamics – how the body moves	Space – where the body moves	Relationships – with whom/ what we move
Whole body actions Stepping Travelling Jumping Turning Gesture Stillness	Quick Slow	**Space** Personal (own), working on the spot General, working all over the room	**Teacher** Near to Away from Around Doing the same as Doing the opposite to Following

The body can also:
bend
stretch
twist
open
close
extend
contract
	Strong
	Light
		Size of movement
		Large
		Small
		Near
		Far
			The class
			Working:
			  individually
			  alongside others
			  cooperatively

Body parts (e.g., head, shoulders, arms, elbows, wrists, hands, fingers, hips, legs, knees, ankles, feet, toes and so on)	Straight Roundabout	**Levels** Low Medium High	**Parts of the body** **Partners** Matching Shadowing Mirroring Question and answer Leader and follower Doing the opposite Meet and part Pass by Travel around

Body parts can:
move individually
  successively
  simultaneously
 	
lead the movement
	Stopping
	Continuous
		Directions
		Forwards
		Backwards
		Sideways
		Upwards
		Downwards
		Diagonally
			Groups
			Small (e.g., trio)
			Large
			Changing shapes
			Changing formations
			Moving in unison
			  or in canon

Body shapes Wide Narrow Round Twisted Symmetrical Asymmetrical		**Patterns and pathways** On the floor In the air Straight Curved Twisted Angular	

Using the movement content chart

The movement content described above has been laid out as a photocopiable chart in four columns, for easy reference (see page 20). Selecting one or two ideas from each or some of the columns, depending on the age and ability of the class, should give a good balance of movement content for a dance idea and can be used as a starting point for planning a dance lesson as well as linking it with a stimulus or topic.

Each of the lesson examples provided has been built around specific movement content which has been selected as appropriate for the particular age group. Any lesson planning needs to consider both the age and experience of the children; for example, in dance, it would be inappropriate to ask five-year-old children to relate to partners, as at this age they are, and need to be, concerned with what they are doing themselves. The complex processes involved in observing a partner and being able to copy the partner exactly would be far too difficult for this age group and would be more appropriate for children aged eight years. Expectations of what would be appropriate movement content for children aged five to seven years (in Key Stage 1) and for seven to eleven years (in Key Stage 2) are indicated on the photocopiable chart outlining progression in dance across the key stages (see page 22).

Progression in dance

It is important to understand progression in dance; that is, how a particular strand in movement is developed from one key stage to the next.

Pupils should be involved in the continuous process of composing, performing and appreciating; although the emphasis of the curriculum is on performing, progression in all three of these processes is important. The end of key stage statements provide a framework for progression in dance. To help teachers understand progression we have devised the chart on page 22, which demonstrates how a particular strand in movement is developed from one key stage to the next. This chart is closely related to and expands upon the programmes of study for dance. However, it is *not* a direct quote from the National Curriculum documents, the Scottish guidelines or the Northern Ireland curriculum.

To develop a particular strand of movement, it is important to take into consideration the age, ability and previous experience of all the children. When planning for progression the difficulty, complexity and the quality of movement needs to be taken into account. The children need to progress from simple tasks to more complex or difficult ones. For example, they should progress from moving on their own, to working with partners, to working in small groups; and from travelling and stopping, to travelling and changing direction, to travelling and changing direction, level and speed.

Progression should be planned. The DES proposals given in *Physical Education for Ages 5 to 16* (1991) identify the following principles of progression:

'Pupils generally move from:
• dependence to independence in learning;
• performing given tasks to being able to structure their own;
• using given criteria to judge others' performance to developing their own criteria to evaluate their and others' performance;
• simple tasks to difficult and complex ones; and
• natural movements to skilful/artistic technical performance.'

Progression in dance
across Key Stages 1 and 2

Key Stage 1	Key Stage 2
Composing	
• Invent, select and adapt a simple phrase.	• Explore, invent, select and refine dance movements.
• Show a clear beginning, middle and an end.	• Shape a simple dance with a clear structure.
• Experience a range of stimuli with an emphasis on music.	• Respond to a range of stimuli: words, poetry, music, sound, pictures, objects and create simple characters and narratives.
• Create movements to show moods and feelings.	• Create dances which communicate feelings, moods and ideas.
Performing	
• Prepare the body before moving.	• Prepare the body to dance.
• Develop control co-ordination balance and poise.	• Control movements varying size, tension and continuity.
• Travelling, stepping, jumping, turning, gesture.	• Link body actions.
• Contrast between movement and stillness.	• Isolate body parts.
• Contrast between large and small shapes.	• Use narrow, wide, curled, twisted, extended and contracted body shapes.
• Demonstrate the difference between fast and slow movements and between strong and light movements.	• Show quality of movement with a range of dynamics.
• Move forwards, backwards and sideways.	• Use different directions including diagonals.
• Move high and low.	• Make changes of level.
• Show an awareness of personal and general space.	• Make patterns and pathways, on the floor and in the air.
• Relate moving to and from the teacher.	• Work with a partner.
• Copy and contrast teacher's movements.	• Work in small groups.
• Work without interfering with others.	• Work as a whole class.
• Respond to simple rhythms.	• Perform and appreciate a variety of rhythms.
• Perform a simple pattern or phrase.	• Perform and repeat simple dance phrases.
• Use of repetition.	
• Perform movements to show moods and feelings.	• Perform dances which communicate feelings, moods and ideas.
• Perform simple traditional folk dances.	• Experience a number of dance forms from different times and places, including some traditional dances of the British Isles.
Appreciating	
• Be aware of different ways of dancing.	
• Observe and describe using appropriate dance vocabulary.	• Use appropriate vocabulary to describe dance.
• Express personal preferences.	• Appreciate in simple terms the aesthetic quality of dance.
• Show simple ways of recording dance.	• Show different ways of recording dance.
• Show sensitivity towards others when watching dance.	• Show sensitivity when appraising others.
• Be aware of the importance of preparing the body before moving.	• Understand the importance of preparing the body to dance.

Stimuli for dance

Dances can be created in many ways using a variety of stimuli. Sometimes the stimulus comes first, sometimes a movement idea is explored and then the stimulus is introduced. There are many sources of stimuli: from movement itself, literary sources, visual sources, aural sources, sources from the senses, from the environment and from topical ideas.

At Key Stage 1 pupils should experience working with a range and variety of contrasting stimuli with an emphasis on music. At Key Stage 2, pupils should respond to music and a range of stimuli, express feelings, moods and ideas, and create simple characters and narratives through dance.

Stimuli may be used as starting points for dance ideas only, they may influence the whole lesson, or they may influence the whole curriculum through the topic or theme.

When imagery is used as a stimulus, it is better to explore the movement possibilities first before mentioning the image, otherwise the children will have preconceived ideas which will limit their movement responses. This approach avoids the idea of the children *being* the image, as opposed to using the movement qualities of the image.

For example, see the 'Jack Frost' lesson on page 61 (Chapter 5, 'Winter') where the children are asked to try running into spaces and to explore making spiky shapes in a variety of ways before they are told that these activities are related to the image of 'Jack Frost'. The same movement experiences could equally relate to 'jagged rocks', for example.

Examples of stimuli can be selected from many sources:
• movement content – that is, body actions, dynamics, space and relationships;
• literary – for example, action words, poems and rhymes, stories and dramatic situations such as newspaper reports and plays, myths and legends;
• visual – for example, objects (such as balloons, shells, mobiles and so on) or props (such as chairs, hats, sunglasses, shoes and scarves) or paintings, photographs, sculptures or videos;
• aural – for example using the voice, body sounds (such as clapping, finger clicks or stamping), percussion, metal, wood or skin instruments or other musical instruments including keyboard, wind and brass or pre-recorded music;
• the senses – that is touch, hearing, smell, taste, sight and the imagination;
• the environment – both natural (for example the weather, growth, planets, water, fire and so on) and manufactured (for example fireworks, machines or buildings);
• topical ideas – such as festivals, seasonal events, celebrations or everyday activities.

The following examples show how dances can be created using some of these different stimuli.

Movement content

Dances can be made by choosing a movement starting point. For example, the children could travel and turn, and meet and part with their partners without any other stimulus, or they could make up their own rhythmic step pattern using a variety of levels, sizes of step and speed, or they could draw simple patterns in the air as shown in the activity, 'The seashore' on page 78 in Chapter 7, 'Summer'.

Action words

Dances can be made using action words as the basis. The children may not be familiar with the meanings of the words. However, true understanding of the meanings of the words and the movements they inspire will come from doing the action over and over again. There is a list of action words provided at the beginning of every lesson in this book. These words can be used as a starting point for a lesson, to extend the movement ideas within the lesson, to develop clarity and quality of movement, or to assist the teacher in providing a rich vocabulary to use during the lesson.

There are five basic body actions: stepping, travelling, jumping, turning and gesture. These, together with stillness, can be expanded upon to translate everyday words into expressive movement. Words can also arise from movement. There should be constant interplay between language and movement, where the one enriches the other. Consequently, the children become interested in words that describe their movement.

For example, the movement word 'turning' could be explored in a variety of ways: high or low; quick or slow; on the spot or travelling; through changing levels; by moving outwards and inwards; on one foot or on two feet; by using hands and feet or by moving on other body parts. All of these actions could be described as: spinning, whirling, twirling, whipping, rotating, swivelling, tumbling, rolling, spiralling, swirling, revolving, stirring, circling or pivoting and so on.

To use action words as a stimulus, begin by making a list of all the action words that you and the children can think of related to the topic. Select three or four of the words from your list to form a phrase, as for 'Kites', page 112, in Chapter 10, 'Air', for example, where the action words selected were: 'soaring, tossing, gliding and falling.' Encourage the children to make a rhythmic phrase by repeating the words several times in any order, for example: 'soar, toss, toss, glide, fall, glide, fall'. This example would be appropriate for Key Stage 2 children, however the phrase is far too long and complex for younger children. Any of the movement ideas on the dance-specific topic webs can be developed in this way.

Poems and rhymes

Poems and rhymes can provide rich sources of ideas for movement and can be used in many ways. Words and phrases can be selected as starting points for the movement. Some poetry will stimulate the actual actions that can be used, such as jumping or turning in the poem 'Ready steady go' in *Look! Look what I Can Do!* by Kate Harrison (1986, BBC) – '... Jumping! Jumping! Touch the sky! ...' and '... Turning slowly, round and round ...'. Some will suggest how to move, for example slowly, as suggested by 'Fog' by Frances Horner in *This Way and That: Poetry for creative dance* edited by F. Baldwin and M. Whitehead (Chatto and Windus, 1972) – '...slowly it creeps on, and on...', while others may suggest a particular mood or an atmosphere. The rhythm of the poem may be used to accompany the dance, and sometimes the whole poem can be used for the performance such as 'Lord of the dance' by Sydney Carter, also in *This Way and That.* Children can use poetry in dance in many ways: they can dance to the whole or part of a poem being recited, or to one of the verses alone or they might say a phrase or word to highlight a movement or they may be able to use their own creative writing as stimuli.

The poem on this page shows the sorts of words or imagery which you might choose as a stimulus to convey movement or images: 'smooth sands', 'spread open', 'approaching sea', 'meet and linger', 'their conversation never ends', 'ensnare the invader', 'jagged and threatening', or 'stand their ground'.

The sea and the shore

Golden smooth sands,
Lie spread open, inviting
The gentle approaching sea.
They meet and linger,
But an unseen hand
Once again separates them.
Their conversation never ends,
For it never has time to begin,
Yet it does not matter.

Little coral basins,
Make much more effort
To ensnare the invader.
Like a mischievous child
Removing a stopper,
The unseen hand lets it out.
Their conversation in passing,
Is flirtatious and flippant,
Trivial as at a cocktail party.

Dark angry rocks,
Jagged and threatening,
Ready for armed combat,
Stand their ground
Against repeated attacks
Of hateful resentment.
The barrage is maintained
Until the unseen hand,
Sensing destruction, separates them.

Edith M. Stokes

Popular chants, such as playground skipping games (see Chapter 16, 'Time and Change', on page 166), rhymes and advertising slogans can also be rich sources for dance. These have a definite metre or rhythm which the children can pick up easily, remember and repeat. Very soon the words will be forgotten and the emphasis will be on how to repeat the rhythm. Children love repetition, new movements and new words. A chant is made up by repeating a word or phrase until a rhythmical pattern emerges; for example, 'Rain, rain, go away! Come again another day!' or 'Snap! Crackle! Pop! Snap! Crackle! Pop!'

Stories

Stories can also provide a wealth of inspiration for dance. The stories used need to be appropriate for the age range of the children. There are many ways of using stories for dance with children, but it is important that the dance does not become drama or mime. For example, the idea of hiding could be developed into a dance. The children could be encouraged to hide behind an imaginary shape and think about how this will influence their body shapes – if they are hiding behind a tall, thin shape then they will need to make themselves as tall and as thin as possible. This could be developed by partner work, with one child making a shape for her partner to hide behind – see 'In the Wild Wood', on page 148, which uses material from Kenneth Grahame's *The Wind in the Willows* (1908, Methuen Children's Books). The same hiding idea could be used at Key Stage 2, using as the stimulus the part of Roald Dahl's *The BFG* (1982, Cape) where Sophie hides in the snozcumber.

Objects

Objects can be used as stimuli for the dance and then discarded or they can be incorporated into the actual dance where they become props. The children can respond to the shape, function, texture, or movement of an object. For example, in 'Balloons', page 106, in Chapter 10, 'Air', the children use the way the balloon gets bigger as it is inflated, and this is then developed into how the balloon moves.

Paintings and photographs

Pictures may provide ideas directly for movement. For example, in Brueghel's painting, *Children's Games*, children are involved in various street games. Elements from the painting could be contrasted with street games today. Pictures of machinery or the mechanism of a watch or clock may suggest turning, spinning and rotating as the cog wheels interlink (see Chapter 13, 'Machines', on page 131). Pictures could be collected from magazines and newspapers for the children to make a collage which could then be used as a stimulus for dance. Images of power or sporting actions translate easily into movement. The children could also use their own paintings showing patterns, shapes, colour, lines or landscapes for inspiration.

Sculpture

The actual shape and form of a sculpture may be used as a starting point for movement or the sculpture may show the final shape and the dance could be built around the creation of this shape. Ideas could be developed individually, with the children gradually changing their body shapes from one shape to the next, or in groups, where one child makes an initial shape and the others in the group have to fit in or relate to the shape.

Video

The use of video is becoming increasingly popular as a stimulus for dance; for example, for younger pupils, the opening sequence of Jim Kylan's *L'Enfant et Les Sortilèges* (1984), as mentioned in *Dance Composition: A practical guide for teachers* by Jacqueline Smith-Autard (1985, Black). In this piece, a young boy is depicted as angry and bad-tempered, which would provide a good means of initiating work. You should make repeated reference to the video encouraging the children to see different aspects: the kinds and quality of movement and the expression conveyed, the use of the music, and the relationship of the dancer to any objects or other people on stage. Another example to show the children would be the dance, *The Simple Man,* after the style of the painter Lowry. There are several ideas within this dance which could be developed: bringing the street to life, looking at the rhythmic step patterns as in the clog dance, taking on the different characters seen in the dance and so on.

Videos can also be used to

look at different dance styles from history and from other cultures, which can then be used as starting points too. For example, the children could look at a video of classical Indian dance and then develop the use of hand gestures as a stimulus for creating their own hand dance (see Chapter 17, 'People and places', on page 167), or they could observe a Pavane from the court of Queen Elizabeth I and use the type of steps, patterns and pathways which they have seen to make up their own Pavan (see Chapter 16, 'Time and change', on page 159). This is a good example to link into history Key Stage 2, Core Study Unit 2: Tudor and Stuart times.

Voice and sound

A whole range of sounds can be created using the voice or by using parts of the body touching other parts of the body, or the floor, to produce clicks, claps, stamps and so on. The children's movements may reflect the quality and the length of the sound: that is, the movement has to fit the sound. Alternatively, a task could be given where the sound has to fit the action. A popular example of this is using vocal sounds to accompany the movement ideas associated with fireworks (see 'Fireworks' on page 54, in Chapter 4, 'Autumn'). Other examples might be vocal sounds to accompany dances about machines, springs, cogs, pistons and levers (see Chapter 13, 'Machines', on page 131) or vocal and body sounds to accompany the movement of a bush fire, a garden bonfire or an erupting volcano (see Chapter 9, 'Fire', on page 97).

Percussion

Each percussion instrument gives a different quality of sound. Metal instruments are continuous, flowing and ongoing; for example the cymbal, triangle, gong or bells. Wooden instruments are sharp, jerky, sudden, staccato; for example, claves, wood blocks, maracas or castanets. Skin instruments are rhythmic; for example a tambour, drums or tambourine.

Percussion instruments can be used to create individual sounds and rhythms; as an accompaniment to the dance or as part of the dance. The instrument may provide musical variation by using changes in volume (loud and quiet), in pitch (high and low) and in rhythm. The tone of a drum or tambour, for example, can be varied by using different beaters, by striking the instrument in different ways (for example tapping with fingers or by the brush of a hand) or by striking different places on the instrument (such as the rim of the tambourine).

Percussion is particularly useful for developing quality in movement. For example, if a sudden, jerky sound were played on the claves the children might respond with a sudden, jerky movement. However, if the rhythm were played on a triangle, the children might respond with light, ongoing movements. The use of percussion may also stimulate an interest in rhythmic patterns. These patterns can be created on the instruments and then the children can move to them, or the movement may influence the rhythms developed.

The children may also become interested in making their own percussion instruments; for example, tins filled with beans to make shakers, rubber bands stretched across a board to pluck or cardboard boxes to beat like drums.

Music

Pre-recorded music can be used as a stimulus in many different ways:
• for rhythm,
• for structure,
• to develop a background mood or atmosphere.

For many people the link between music and dance is so strong that they feel there has to be music if there is to be dance. Finding the right piece of music is always difficult and often, because teachers could not find suitable pieces of music, dance has just not taken place. Music, of course, does have strong links with dance, but it is possible for children to dance to a number of other accompaniments such as poems, body sounds or percussion and dance can also take place in silence.

Where music is used as a stimulus, it may influence the movement response directly; for example lively, quick music may result in the children moving in this way. Similarly slow calming music should influence the way the children respond.

Music may be selected for its rhythm. Young children could be asked to march to

brass band music or step patterns could be created to African drumming or the sound of the tabla used in Asian dancing. This can provide an excellent opportunity for teachers to raise children's awareness of different rhythms, as well as the sound of instruments from different cultures.

Music can also be selected because of its structure; for example the music to a song may have a verse, chorus, verse, chorus (ABAB) structure. This can be used to aid the choreographic structure of the dance; for example, each time the chorus is repeated the children could return to their particular movement phrase and repeat it. This provides a certain security for the children, knowing that they are always going to return to a familiar section of the dance.

Music can be used to stimulate movement, as suggested, but it an also be used to accompany the movement. The choice of music depends on how it is to be used, but also the length and complexity of the music needs to be considered. It is better to use short simple pieces of music with younger children. It is difficult to recommend suitable pieces as the choice of music is very personal and what appeals to one teacher and class may not be suitable in another situation. It is not recommended that you use pop music all of the time, as it is repetitive and children associate it with disco dancing, which limits their creative responses. You will need to build up a class or whole-school resource bank of suitable music, together with suggestions of how the music might be useful. Photocopiable page 176 has been included at the end of this book to encourage teachers to make up their own resource list for their school. Encourage colleagues to exchange music that they have found worked well.

When the music has been selected it is useful to tape it several times to allow you to become familiar with it and in the lesson enable you to ask the children to repeat their movement phrases and the dance ideas they are working on without having to constantly rewind the tape.

Using the senses
In addition to visual and auditory stimuli, tactile stimuli can be another source for movement ideas. Something smooth and soft, such as a piece of velvet or a silk scarf, will create a very different response to something sharp and spiky, such as a sea urchin or a piece of coral. Imagery is often used in dance, but, as stated earlier, it is important that the children are given the opportunity to explore the movement ideas first before introducing the image to avoid a purely mimetic response or the idea of 'being' the image.

Using topical ideas, festivals and celebrations
These provide a wide source of ideas for dance and there are several examples provided in the lessons in this book, for example, 'Spring-cleaning' in Chapter 15, 'Stories', and 'Fireworks' in Chapter 4, 'Autumn'. Events such as the January sales suggest immediate ideas: crowds, queuing, rushing, pushing, sorting, moving up and down the escalators and so on. Festivals and celebrations provide ideal opportunities to also look at other cultures through their traditions; for example: Diwali, the Hindu/Sikh festival of light; Harvest, considering sowing, reaping, winnowing, grinding and sifting; Christmas, exploring wrapping presents with folding, rolling and creasing movements; the Chinese New Year, typified by firecrackers and dragons; Pancake Day with the mixing and tossing of pancakes; or May Day, traditionally celebrated by maypole and morris dancing.

The environment
The immediate environment with which the children are familiar can prove to be a valuable resource. If possible, take the children out of the classroom to explore the school surroundings; go for a walk, organise a trip to the nearest park, village or town, to a farm or into the country or to the seaside. For example, the children might explore mapping a journey from home to school thinking about pathways and directions (see page 124 in Chapter 12, 'Patterns'). The skyline may create ideas for varying levels and shapes in groups. Patterns on buildings and their structures can influence body

shape. Exploring different environments further afield, both real or imaginary, can be used. Different seasonal and geographical landscapes can influence group work; the soft lines and the changing contours of a winter landscape or the strong, solid, rugged, mountain ranges and peaks or the rainforests and deserts or changing seascapes of the world under the sea. Imaginary journeys to outer space, to explore the galaxy and different planets and terrains can produce exciting movement material: a slippery planet, a cold planet or a planet with holes and craters for going over, under and through.

Structuring a dance

In order to create or shape or structure a dance, movement ideas or motifs, based on the initial stimulus can be linked together to create phrases. These can range in length from one or two movements to a longer dance with two or more clear sections. Variation in the dance can be created by developing the basic motif. For example, part of the original motif may be enlarged or reduced (as suggested in the lesson 'Spring-cleaning' in Chapter 15, 'Stories', on page 152), or the motif may be performed on the spot and then enlarged so that the children are using the whole space (as suggested in the lesson 'The seashore' in Chapter 7, 'Summer', on page 78). Changes can also be made to the levels or directions used.

The same basic motif can be developed by using the right-hand side of the body first and then the left-hand side of the body or it can be performed using a totally different part of the body.

The actual order or sequence of movements contained in the original motif can be changed too, for example the ideas could be performed in reverse order. The use of repetition is very important in constructing and creating dances as it can emphasise what is being 'said' in the movements. Similarly, the use of contrast can be very effective. Dance is concerned with movement and action, but including stillness in a dance can be very effective and can make a strong statement.

All dances, however long, should have a clear beginning, middle and end, so that the children know how their dance starts, the sequence of their dance movements and how their dance finishes. This arrangement of the phrases into a repeatable dance is the beginning of 'form' in dance.

CHAPTER 2

Lesson planning

Using a topic-based approach

There are several ways of teaching dance, but for the non-specialist we believe that teaching through a topic-based approach is probably one of the most accessible. Also, it is a way of incorporating dance into an already overloaded curriculum. Most primary schools still base their curriculum planning around a broad topic, even when using a subject-based model. For example, topics such as 'Materials', 'Water' and 'Weather' will be familiar to most primary teachers.

The planning process involves four steps:
• Step one: Cross-curricular brainstorming;
• Step two: Constructing a dance-specific topic web;
• Step three: Choosing a stimulus;
• Step four: Deciding on the movement content.

To help you through the stages of planning a lesson, these four steps have been outlined below in detail, using the example of 'The weather' as the topic. However, this planning process can be used to plan any dance topic.

The diagrams show the sorts of webs you might produce at each stage, although your particular situation and environment and the children's experience and classroom work will influence significantly the content of each web.

If 'The weather' is the broad topic that the school has selected to work on, then an example of a topic web identifying all the related curriculum areas might look like the one which has been included below. From this,

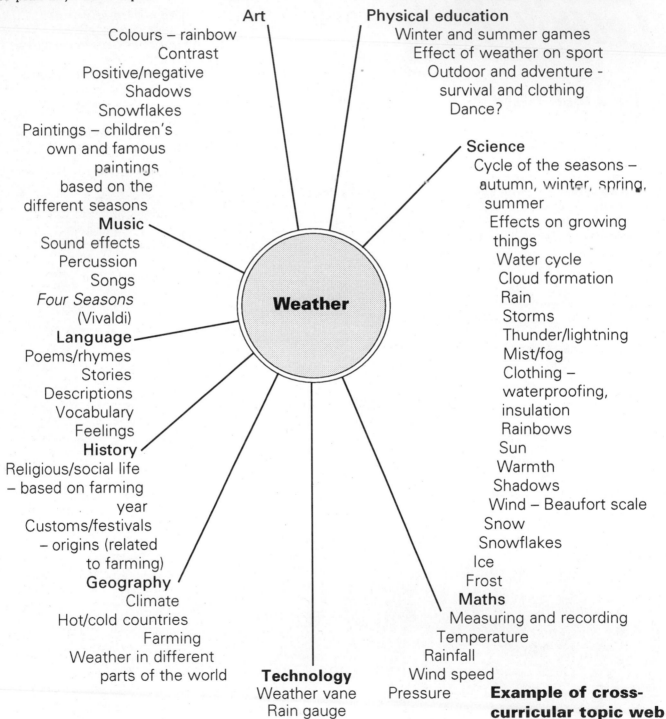

Art
Colours – rainbow
Contrast
Positive/negative
Shadows
Snowflakes
Paintings – children's
own and famous
paintings
based on the
different seasons

Music
Sound effects
Percussion
Songs
Four Seasons
(Vivaldi)

Language
Poems/rhymes
Stories
Descriptions
Vocabulary
Feelings

History
Religious/social life
– based on farming
year
Customs/festivals
– origins (related
to farming)

Geography
Climate
Hot/cold countries
Farming
Weather in different
parts of the world

Physical education
Winter and summer games
Effect of weather on sport
Outdoor and adventure -
survival and clothing
Dance?

Science
Cycle of the seasons –
autumn, winter, spring,
summer
Effects on growing
things
Water cycle
Cloud formation
Rain
Storms
Thunder/lightning
Mist/fog
Clothing –
waterproofing,
insulation
Rainbows
Sun
Warmth
Shadows
Wind – Beaufort scale
Snow
Snowflakes
Ice
Frost

Maths
Measuring and recording
Temperature
Rainfall
Wind speed
Pressure

Technology
Weather vane
Rain gauge

Weather

Example of cross-curricular topic web

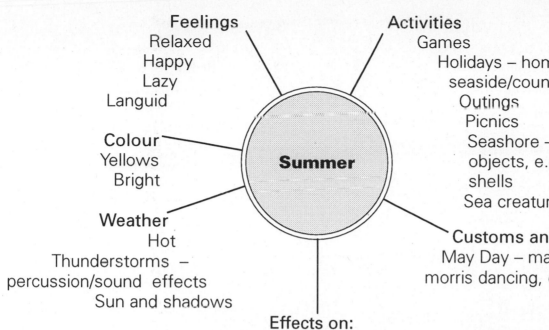

Feelings
Relaxed
Happy
Lazy
Languid

Colour
Yellows
Bright

Weather
Hot
Thunderstorms –
percussion/sound effects
Sun and shadows

Summer

Activities
Games
Holidays – home/abroad,
seaside/country
Outings
Picnics
Seashore – natural
objects, e.g., seaweed,
shells
Sea creatures

Customs and festivals
May Day – maypole and
morris dancing, carnivals

Effects on:
Nature – flowers, animals
People – clothing, e.g., sun-
glasses, sandals/bare feet, hats

Example of dance-specific topic web

'Summer' (as part of the 'Cycle of seasons') has been identified as a focus for the class and a dance-specific topic web developed (see above). The diagram on page 34 shows how the four areas of the movement content have been considered for this dance lesson with reference to the stimulus and the age and ability of the class concerned.

Step one: Cross-curricular brainstorming
Any topic work needs careful planning. One of the many ways is to begin by 'brainstorming' for the chosen topic around the whole curriculum, identifying the possible content to be included under all subject areas. You will probably be familiar with this way of planning to incorporate either all areas of the curriculum or two or three subject areas on

which you have chosen to focus. After this initial brainstorming a topic web, like the one shown below for 'Weather', is created, identifying all the curriculum areas to be included.

Unless you already have the knowledge, skills and understanding in dance it can prove difficult when trying to see how to include dance in the topic web. However, there are often movement ideas in other subject areas which can be used for dance and their potential should not be overlooked. For example, on a topic web for 'Weather', thunder and lightning might have been identified under science. This is an idea which could be used for dance by using whole body movements travelling through space such as rolling and jumping, using the contrast of heavy, slow movements and light, nimble, quick movements.

Step two: Constructing a dance-specific topic web
Having completed the cross-curricular brainstorming for a topic, the next step in planning the dance content is to draw out all the possible ideas that could be developed into movement to create a dance-specific topic web. In the example of 'The weather', the seasons cycle has been identified under science. This would include the four seasons of autumn, winter, spring, summer. If we take 'Summer' as our example, the next step would be to create a dance-specific topic web on 'Summer'. The 'Summer' dance-specific web above was created from the cross-curricular web shown on page 32. By comparison, you will see which ideas have been selected which could then be developed into dance.

Step three: Choosing a stimulus
You must now select one idea from your dance-specific web and try to think of a stimulus or starting point, linked to the

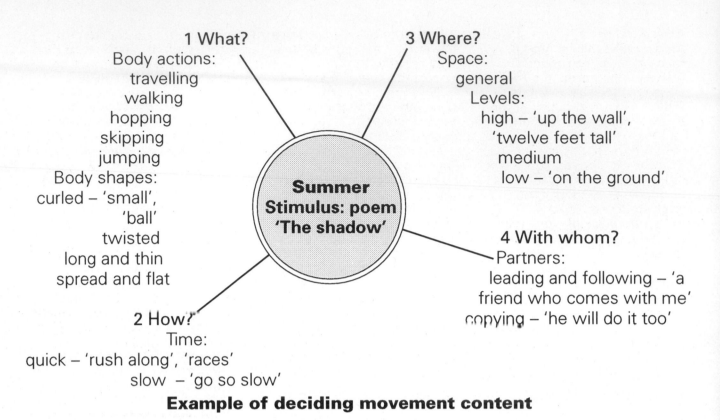

1 What?
Body actions:
  travelling
  walking
  hopping
  skipping
  jumping
Body shapes:
curled – 'small',
  'ball'
  twisted
long and thin
spread and flat

Summer Stimulus: poem 'The shadow'

3 Where?
Space:
  general
  Levels:
   high – 'up the wall',
    'twelve feet tall'
   medium
    low – 'on the ground'

4 With whom?
Partners:
  leading and following – 'a friend who comes with me'
  copying – 'he will do it too'

2 How?
Time:
quick – 'rush along', 'races'
  slow – 'go so slow'

Example of deciding movement content

topic, which is appropriate to the age and ability of the children. It may be a poem, a piece of music, an object or a story. Try to use a range of stimuli with the children and not just music. For example, in Chapter 7, 'Summer', the poem 'The shadow' has been chosen for the seven to nine years age group (see page 82) because the vocabulary, the language and the movement ideas used are appropriate to the age of the children.

Step four: Deciding on the movement content
Next you must decide on the movement content the children need to experience. This can be selected by using the photocopiable chart on page 20, as shown in the diagram above.

Consider the four movement content areas, starting with the 'What?'. In the case of the poem, 'The shadow', the body

actions are suggested by the phrases of the poem such as travelling: 'I rush along with huge great paces,' and body shapes such as curled: 'I curl myself up like a ball' or long and thin: 'I stretch right out all long and thin'. These phrases have been selected because they directly link with the body action and body shape ideas mentioned in the poem.

When considering 'How?' the children will move, the contrast of moving quickly and slowly has been selected, inspired by the phrases: 'But he comes too – in fact, he races' and 'I test him out, and go so slow'.

For the 'Where?', the poem suggests using the general space and travelling anywhere within it: 'On sunny days I am never free' and using different levels: 'On the ground or up the wall'.

Finally, when considering the relationships involved,

working with partners was selected; also based on the poem: 'For I have a friend who comes with me'.

To help with planning topics in this way a photocopiable page is provided on page 177. The completed ideas sheets can be kept as a resource for future dance lesson planning.

Lesson structure
Once you have decided on a dance idea, chosen a stimulus and selected the movement content you want the children to experience, you need to consider the structure of the dance lessons and how long it will take to develop the ideas.

The plan for any dance lesson should have an introduction to the dance idea, an opportunity to explore and develop the movement ideas and using the stimulus create, perform and appreciate dances.

Introduction

All dance lessons should be focused by an introductory activity which prepares the class for the work which is to follow. This might start in the classroom by talking about and discussing with the children the dance ideas and how they might develop them, linking in with other subjects or ongoing topics, or you might follow on from a particular piece of work that has been produced in class, for example a child's poem may be the starting point for a dance lesson. You might discuss the content of the previous dance lesson and what the class are going on to next. It is essential that you prepare the children for the lesson by creating the right mood and atmosphere to enable them to relate to you, the teacher, and help them to listen and concentrate. This can easily be achieved through the music selected. The children should learn to and understand why they need to prepare their bodies to move.

All children should participate in warm-up activities so that they are able to:
• raise their heartbeats;
• develop and improve the flexibility and suppleness in their whole bodies and parts of their bodies;
• develop and increase stamina.

These warm-up activities should be fun and, where possible, should link to the main movement content and ideas in the lesson. The introduction should include vigorous whole body actions such as running, skipping, galloping, bending, stretching, twisting and turning and the movement of body parts, on the spot and leading into travelling and jumping, after warming-up the feet and ankles. These warm up activities can be linked together to create rhythmical phrases using music or percussion to accompany them where appropriate. The warm-up should be integrated into the lesson, if possible, so that the whole lesson flows from one section to the next.

Movement development

In this part of the lesson the main aspects of the movement content selected for the dance are experienced, explored and developed in a variety of ways using repetition and contrast. The work should include an awareness of body action, dynamics, space and relationships (see 'Movement content' in Chapter 1, 'The language of dance', on page 16), expression of feelings, ideas and meaning and should develop, and flow on from, the movement experienced during the introduction to the lesson.

Dance idea

The individual movement experiences are now related to the chosen stimuli, for example music can be introduced here or the movement experiences may be enhanced through the use of imagery. Always use imagery to describe movements; for example, do not ask the children to *be* a balloon, a flower or a cat, but use the movement images such as the expanding and drifting of a balloon, the opening and closing of a flower, or the creeping and pouncing movements of a cat. This will enable the children to broaden their movement vocabulary and not have any preconceived ideas on how to move. The children then select from their ideas to create dances on their own, with partners, or in small groups. Dances should have a clear structure with a beginning, a middle and an end, that can be remembered, repeated and shared with others. The children should be encouraged to watch, comment on and appreciate each others work.

Although we have divided the lesson structure into three sections, they should not be seen as distinct but as a whole, flowing from one to the other. Each section may vary in length, depending on the initial idea and where the class are in creating their dance. For example, in a unit of work for four weeks, in week one you might spend more time on introducing and exploring ideas, while in week two you might concentrate on selecting ideas and in week three spend more time on creating a dance and in week four work on perfecting, performing, sharing and appreciating that dance.

The length and number of lessons in a unit will vary depending on the age and ability of the class. At the beginning of Key Stage 1 lessons should last approximately 20 minutes building up to 30 minutes by the end of Key Stage 2. At Key Stage 1 you might work on a dance idea for one, two or three lessons, but by Key Stage 2 a dance idea could be developed over four or even six weeks.

Preparation for dance

Before starting to dance a number of basic requirements and safety procedures need to be considered.

Space

For the children to dance a space is required The space available in the majority of primary schools is usually a multi-purpose hall which is used for assemblies, gymnastics, drama, music, watching television, eating lunches and so on. It is important you ensure that the hall is prepared in advance and is safe for the children to use to move in.

The floor needs to be clean and non-slip. You should be aware of any items of furniture (such as the piano, stage blocks, dining furniture, television and cables) and where these may be a hazard they need to be moved to the side or even removed altogether.

In a small school there may not be a hall. This should not deter you or deny the children access to dance. A classroom can be used by moving the chairs and tables to the sides of the room.

Clothes

It is essential that the children change their clothes for the lesson and understand why particular clothing should be worn and the risks of wearing inappropriate clothing. The children should have a change of clothing for reasons of hygiene, but changing also provides an opportunity for young children to dress, undress and prepare themselves for a physical activity.

Clothing should be 'comfortable' enabling the children to move without any restrictions. Suitable clothing might be vests and pants for infants and for junior children, T-shirts and shorts or cotton leggings, or leotards may be worn. It is not suitable for the children to wear school uniform, training shoes or outdoor shoes for dance. Not only is this unhygienic and unsafe, but the children would be unable to roll on the floor, for example, and their movement would be restricted. Also this type of clothing would make it difficult to appreciate the line of the dance.

It is recommended that the children dance with bare feet, to encourage them to use the whole of each foot, including the toes, heels and sides of the feet. This enables the children to flex and extend their ankles and feet. This is important for safety reasons in preparation for jumping and landing, as well as being healthy exercise for the feet. Also, bare feet will enhance the sensitivity and quality of the movement and extension through the whole body. However, if a child has a foot infection and needs to wear shoes, then these should be flexible-soled plimsolls.

Jewellery

For safety purposes, all jewellery *must* be removed before the children dance. In a multicultural society this can be a sensitive issue as certain pieces of jewellery have cultural and religious significance. However, many potential problems can be overcome; for example, the Kara (a steel bangle) worn by Sikh boys can be covered by wearing a sweat band, rather than causing distress by asking the boys to remove their Karas.

Accident procedure

In the event of an accident the teacher and children should be familiar with the appropriate accident procedures in their school. There is usually someone on the staff who has followed a suitable course and is responsible for first aid provision. If an accident does occur during a dance lesson, send for this qualified person, rather than trying to deal with the situation yourself which may compound the problem. All schools should have clear, strict guidelines on this matter. It is also important that you are aware of individual medical conditions and are able to deal with them on a day to day basis, as well as in emergency situations.

CHAPTER 3

Assessment in dance

'Assessment is at the heart of the process of promoting children's learning. It can provide a framework in which educational objectives may be set and pupil's progress charted and expressed. It can yield a basis for planning the next educational steps in response to children's needs. By facilitating dialogue between teachers, it can enhance professional skills and help the school as a whole to strengthen learning across the curriculum and throughout its age range.' (DES, Task Group on Assessment and Testing, 1987).

Assessment can help teachers to plan the next stage of learning, to review and evaluate their schemes and units of work and to ensure that learning objectives or intentions are being met. Assessment can also help teachers to identify and focus upon individual children's needs and record the overall achievements of pupils.

Purposes of assessment

'Assessment of pupils' attainment is a continuous process and is integral to all teaching and learning. It will inform teachers and pupils about progress, and help to identify learners' strengths and weaknesses and needs.' (NCC, *Non-Statutory Guidance [Physical Education]*, 1992)

The end of key stage statements provide a framework for making assessment, planning the next stage of learning and reporting to parents. Information gathered during Key Stage 1 can be used to help plan the learning in Key Stage 2 and beyond. It is important that the assessment is seen as a continuous process.

Assessment can also help children to recognise their achievements, to improve their performance and to receive feedback and comments upon their work from both the teacher and other pupils. This involvement of pupils in the assessment process can help to clarify for them the original intention and lead to greater understanding for some children, as well as providing them with the opportunity to make comments and use the correct vocabulary when describing dances they have observed. This is the beginning of critical appraisal in dance.

Assessment also has a purpose when the teacher is reporting to parents. Teachers are required to report against the end of key stage statements. Reports to parents should significantly reflect the positive achievements of the child and provide the parents with a more informed view about how their child is progressing.

Implementing assessment

Assessment should be considered as an integral part of the teaching and learning process and not as something extra. It should *not* be the main purpose of the lesson. If the learning intentions are clearly identified then the assessment should naturally fall into place. Clear learning intentions will promote quality learning, and encourage and support effective practice. The lesson examples in this book provide opportunities for assessment in dance by engaging the children in the three interrelated processes of composing, performing and appreciating. When composing, the children will be using the skills of exploring, inventing, selecting and refining movements, while planning and making their own dances; when performing, they will be using the skills of performing, expressing, projecting, practising and repeating dance phrases; and when appreciating they will be using the skills of observing, interpreting, evaluating and describing using appropriate dance vocabulary.

At the end of each of our lesson examples we have identified, under the headings of 'Composing', 'Performing' and 'Appreciating', a list of progressive statements, extracted in full or in part from the photocopiable chart on page 22, 'Progression across Key Stages 1 and 2'. These statements are closely related to and expand upon the programmes of study for dance and could form the basis of an assessment model.

For example at Key Stage 1, looking at the 'Balloons' lesson in Chapter 10, 'Air', on page 106, you may decide to focus for your assessment on how well the children can respond to simple rhythms. With respect to this, the Programme of Study (Dance) states that 'Pupils should: ...be helped to develop rhythmic responses', while the End of Key Stage

Statement states that by the end of Key Stage 1 'Pupils should be able to: plan and perform safely a range of simple actions in response to given tasks and stimuli,' and the Programme of Study (General) states that 'Pupils should: ...respond to simple rhythms...'. If you read the introduction part of the 'Balloons' lesson, you will see that the children are being asked to try to bounce in time with the rhythm. This is an integral part of the lesson and you will be able to observe how well the children are able to respond to rhythm at this stage in the lesson. You may wish then to record your observations. Examples of how you can record this

information are shown on record sheets on page 44. You may decide initially to focus on just six children, so that your recording does not impede upon the natural pace and timing of the lesson. It is also important that you are seen to be fully involved when teaching the dance lesson, rather than standing on the side with a clipboard. By identifying a particular strand to focus upon for assessment, you will find that it helps you to direct or focus your observations and sharpen your teaching.

At Key Stage 2, you may decide that, for example, you wish to focus on how well the children can create a simple partner dance. For each lesson you will see that several 'Learning outcomes' have been identified as appropriate phrases from the progression chart. For the purposes of assessment, you may select only one statement from each of 'Composing', 'Performing', and 'Appreciating'; for example, looking at the 'Pathways' lesson on page 126 in Chapter 12, 'Patterns': 'Shape a simple dance' (Composing), 'Work with a partner' (Performing), and 'Show simple ways of recording dance' (Appreciating). The dance idea in this particular lesson involves the children in copying each other's step patterns and then asks them to perform their step patterns in different ways, so that various partner situations are experienced. The children are then asked to record on the photocopiable worksheet provided (page 187) the different ways that they worked with their partners.

Then one couple is asked to observe another couple's dance and they are encouraged to describe the way they worked together. As well as having the opportunity to observe the children yourself while they are performing their dance for another couple and vice versa and recording how well they have answered the set task, you will also have the completed photocopiable pages that can be used as evidence for your assessment.

The lesson examples provide plenty of opportunity for you to observe your class as they are moving. Observation is the key to all movement and dance teaching. The ability to observe your class and to react to what you see are fundamental to good teaching, as well as helping you with your assessment of that class. Once a task has

been set, you need to step back and observe the class to see whether they are all answering the set task. Some children may be experiencing difficulty because they did not listen or have genuinely misunderstood what you have asked them to do. Consequently, it may seem necessary for you to repeat the task, perhaps using slightly different phrasing or explaining terminology, just as you would in the classroom where you might say the same thing in several different ways. If the task set is too difficult for the majority of the class then you may need to adapt or modify it in some way. For example, if you have asked them to include changes in level, speed and direction all at once then you may need to break this down stage by stage.

Sometimes using some of the children to show their ideas to the rest of the class can help to clarify the type of responses that you are looking for and this can then prompt others into action. A good demonstration can be an invaluable teaching aid, but again your observation will be necessary when selecting those who will demonstrate. It is usually better to show two or three responses to avoid everyone just copying, or half the class may show their responses while the other half of the class watches. When using a demonstration it is important that all the children can see and that they know exactly what they are looking for. For example, at Key Stage 1 they may be watching for a change of level or who can keep in time with the rhythm. This provides an opportunity for both you and the class to direct your observations against specific criteria. It will help you to observe if the content that you have selected was suitable and if the children are ready to progress as well as providing information for assessment.

Recording achievement

Evidence for assessment can be gathered through observation, through written and oral work, and through the use of video and photographs. Written evidence may be provided by the children's writing about their dances. Some of the photocopiable pages and much of the follow-up work suggested in this book can be used as evidence for assessment. For example, in Chapter 12, 'Patterns', in the Key Stage 1 lesson, 'Journey to school' (page 124), the children are involved in recording their journeys to school by drawing their pathways. These maps can be used by the teacher as evidence of knowledge and understanding and as a means of the children being able to chart their own achievement. Encouraging the children to talk about and comment upon their observations will provide you with an opportunity to acquire oral evidence, for example, of how the dance is structured – does it have a clear beginning and so on.

Listening to the children using appropriate vocabulary and terminology for dance shows evidence of their understanding. Video and photographs provide opportunities for you to look more closely at the children's work; for example, has their dance a beginning, a middle and an end? Are the children showing a variety of body shape? Does the dance show a range of dynamics?

Assessment should not be unduly onerous and should not impinge upon your being fully involved in teaching the dance lesson. It is not necessary to assess all of the pupils all of the time, but any significant evidence should be recorded. For example, when an individual or a group of the children have the ability to demonstrate the difference between fast and slow movements when involved in making up a dance using 'fast and slow', this becomes significant evidence.

Individual schools need to develop their own systems for recording and reporting with which the teachers can become confident and familiar. Record keeping for assessment should be kept to a minimum and should record evidence of pupil's achievements. Records of attainment should be made throughout the key stage and not in isolation. Examples of records of assessment for dance at Key Stages 1 and 2, using example lessons from this book together with the proposed assessment model are given below. A blank photocopiable record sheet is provided on page 178 for individual use.

When using the record sheet:
• list the children's names in the left-hand column;
• write in the class and year in the appropriate places;

• write in the title of unit of work;
• select the learning outcomes on which you wish to focus and write them in the boxes provided, ensuring that you have at least one statement from each of the 'Composing', 'Performing', and 'Appreciating' sections of the progression chart;
• place a tick against each child's name when they achieve each of the learning outcomes you wish to assess.

Attainment target charts

The progression chart on which the learning outcomes and assessment model for this book are based were distilled, primarily,
from the National Curriculum for England and Wales. In order to assist teachers in Scotland and Northern Ireland to make the most of these lesson plans and to help them to tailor and adapt the progression and assessment models and the learning outcomes to their particular situations, charts linking each lesson to the specific curriculum guidelines are included on the following two pages.

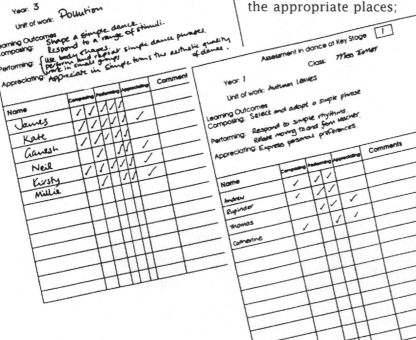

AT CHARTS

Scotland

There are six strands for physical education in the *Expressive Arts 5–14* document. While many of the dance ideas in this book fit loosely into the first three stands, the particular focus is on 'Creating and designing', 'Co-operating, sharing, communicating and competing' and 'Observing, reflecting, describing and responding'. Aspects of the strand 'Using the body' can also be applied to all these dance ideas, but this strand is far more concerned with functional, rather than creative, movement. In the chart below **3**/2 means lesson plan 2 in Chapter 3.

Strand Level	Creating and designing	Co-operating, sharing, communicating and competing	Observing, reflecting, describing and responding
A	4/1, 5/1, 6/1, 7/1, 8/1, 9/1, 10/1, 11/1, 12/1, 13/1, 14/1, 15/1, 16/1, 17/1	4/1, 5/1, 6/1, 7/1, 8/1, 9/1, 10/1, 11/1, 12/1, 13/1, 14/1, 15/1, 16/1, 17/1	4/1, 5/1, 6/1, 7/1, 8/1, 9/1, 10/1, 11/1, 12/1, 13/1, 14/1, 15/1, 16/1, 17/1
B	4/1, 4/2, 5/1, 5/2, 6/1, 6/2, 7/2, 8/2, 9/2, 10/1, 11/2, 12/1, 14/2, 15/1, 15/2, 16/1, 17/1	4/1, 4/2, 5/1, 5/2, 6/1, 6/2, 7/2, 8/2, 9/2, 10/1, 11/2, 12/1, 14/2, 15/2, 17/1	4/1, 4/2, 5/1, 5/2, 6/1, 6/2, 7/2, 8/2, 9/2, 10/1, 11/2, 12/1, 15/2
C	4/2, 5/2, 6/2, 7/2, 8/2, 9/2, 10/2, 11/2, 12/2, 13/2, 14/2, 15/2, 16/2, 17/2	4/2, 5/2, 6/2, 7/2, 8/2, 9/2, 10/2, 11/2, 12/2, 13/2, 14/2, 15/2, 16/2, 17/2	4/2, 5/2, 6/2, 7/2, 8/2, 9/2, 10/2, 11/2, 12/2, 13/2, 15/2, 16/2
D	4/3, 5/3, 6/3, 7/3, 8/3, 9/2, 9/3, 10/2, 10/3, 11/3, 12/2, 12/3, 14/3, 15/3, 16/2, 16/3, 17/2, 17/3	4/3, 5/3, 6/3, 7/3, 8/3, 9/2, 9/3, 10/2, 10/3, 11/3, 12/2, 12/3, 13/3, 14/3, 15/3, 16/2, 16/3, 17/2, 17/3	4/3, 5/3, 6/3, 7/3, 8/3, 9/2, 9/3, 10/2, 10/3, 11/3, 12/2, 12/3, 13/3, 14/3, 15/3, 16/2, 16/3, 17/3
E	4/3, 5/3, 6/3, 7/3, 8/3, 9/3, 10/3, 11/3, 12/3, 13/3, 14/3, 15/3, 16/3, 17/3	4/3, 5/3, 6/3, 7/3, 8/3, 9/3, 10/3, 11/3, 12/3, 13/3, 14/3, 15/3, 16/3, 17/3	4/3, 5/3, 6/3, 7/3, 8/3, 9/3, 10/3, 11/3, 12/3, 13/3, 17/3

Northern Ireland

The chart on this page refers to the *Northern Ireland Common Curriculum in Physical Education*. It can be used to identify the relevant statements of attainment/teaching objectives within the two attainment targets; Performance, and Appraising and Evaluating Performance. In the chart below the coding system **4**/1, meaning Chapter 4 lesson 1, has been employed to indicate suitable teaching material at given levels. The teacher should be aware that particular statements of attainment/ teaching objectives may be predominant at different times in the teaching sequence.

	Statements of Attainment *Teaching objectives – Relating to Dance*	*Lessons*
Level 1 AT1	Pupils should be able to: a) respond appropriately to simple instructions and stimuli; b) perform simple movement tasks in a range of physical activities; c) move safely in the performance of different activities; e) produce some ideas in relation to simple movement tasks.	4/1 9/1 14/1 5/1 10/1 15/1 6/1 11/1 16/1 7/1 12/1 17/1 8/1 13/1
AT2	a) show an awareness of basic body care.	
Level 2 AT1	a) respond and communicate instructions and ideas; b) show controlled movement in the use of space; c) respond in an expressive and inventive manner, individually and with others, to various stimuli.	4/1 9/1 14/1 5/1 10/1 15/1 6/1 11/1 16/1 7/1 12/1 17/1 8/1 13/1
AT2	a) observe and describe their own movements and those of their peers in a range of physical activities; b) recognise and describe some of the effects of activity.	
Level 3 AT1	a) practise skills to promote control and co-ordination of the body, using equipment where appropriate, in a range of activities; b) show poise, control and co-ordination using a range of appropriate actions in the performance of movement; d) co-operate in small groups in the solving of movement problems.	4/2 9/2 14/2 5/2 10/2 15/2 6/2 11/2 16/2 7/2 12/2 17/2 8/2 13/2
AT2	a) observe, describe in different ways and answer questions about the movements of themselves and others; b) show an awareness of the relationship between exercise and physical well-being.	
Level 4 AT1	a) utilise and extend skills to facilitate controlled and co-ordinated performance; b) move with poise, control and co-ordination in response to a variety of stimuli when practising and/or solving tasks both individually and in groups; e) sustain activity for a period of time; f) co-operate in groups in the solving of movement problems.	4/2 9/2 14/2 5/2 10/2 15/2 6/2 11/2 16/2 7/2 12/2 17/2 8/2 13/2
AT2	a) observe and comment upon the movements of themselves and others and being able to recognise good performance in relation to tasks set; b) show an understanding of the relationship between fitness, exercise and physical well-being.	
Level 5 AT1	a) perform skilful and aesthetically pleasing sequences; b) demonstrate skilful performance in co-operative and competitive activities; c) explore through movement the solution to activity tasks in different environments; d) show a responsible approach to safety; e) co-operate in groups to discuss, select and then perform using ideas from other areas of the accompaniment for movement.	4/3 9/3 14/3 5/3 10/3 15/3 6/3 11/3 16/3 7/3 12/3 17/3 8/3 13/3
AT2	a) observe, analyse and suggest ways to improve the movements of themselves and others; b) show an awareness of the effect of exercise on the body; c) show an awareness of the importance of hygiene.	
Level 6 AT1	a) extend, refine and repeat a range of skills in a variety of contexts; b) utilise and develop ideas from other curricula areas as a stimulus or an accompaniment for movement in a variety of contexts; c) demonstrate an awareness of the skills and fitness requirements of a number of physical activities; d) plan and perform effectively in a range of activities.	4/3 9/3 14/3 5/3 10/3 15/3 6/3 11/3 16/3 7/3 12/3 17/3 8/3 13/3
AT2	a) make informed judgements in relation to the personal performance of themselves and others; b) show an understanding of the benefits of exercise to health; c) show an awareness of opportunities provided for participation in sport, leisure and recreation in the community.	

CHAPTER 4

Autumn

The topic of 'Autumn' or particular ideas connected with the time of year (such as: observing how the leaves change colour before falling from the trees and the associated activities of sweeping the leaves up into a heap for a bonfire, the customs of Bonfire Night and firework displays; the weather becoming cooler, autumn mists and the need for warmer clothing for protection from the wind and rain; harvesting the crops and ensuring that they are all gathered in and stored in preparation for the coming winter), all lend themselves particularly to movement and have, therefore, been included on the dance-specific topic web on page 48. This topic also fits in with other topics such as 'The seasons' and 'The weather'and makes specific cross-curricular links with science.

The three example lessons provided in this chapter use the ideas of autumn leaves and fireworks. For the five- to seven-year-old age range, the idea of the autumn leaves falling has been selected and a poem has been used as the stimulus. The children work individually initially using the ideas of the leaves

falling and then being blown by the wind. This idea is developed in the seven- to nine-year-olds' lesson, where the children work in twos as if they are being swirled and tossed by the wind. The chosen stimulus for this lesson is a sound effect of the wind. The lesson for nine- to eleven-year-olds uses the popular imagery of fireworks and the use of the children's own vocal sounds to accompany their movements, until eventually a complete firework display dance is created. Specific follow-up ideas for movement are suggested after each lesson.

Both the ideas used in this chapter can be developed across the curriculum. The life cycle of a leaf could be studied, which would link with science. You might like to suggest that the children collect fallen leaves and then make leaf rubbings, to raise their awareness of the different leaf shapes and the veins in the leaves. Note the colours and compare and contrast the texture of a leaf growing on a branch with a dry leaf that has fallen to the ground. Involving the class in creating wind sound effects, using their own vocal sounds or by using percussion instruments, would also link the topic with music. Cross-curricular links with the 'Fireworks' lesson could involve learning and reinforcing the Firework Code with regards to safety, and researching the historical event of the Gunpowder Plot, which could be used to link this dance work into Key Stage 2 history, Core Study Unit 2: Tudor and Stuart times. After the dance lesson, the children could either write about or paint a picture of the 'firework display' dance that they observed or their own group display.

ACTIVITIES

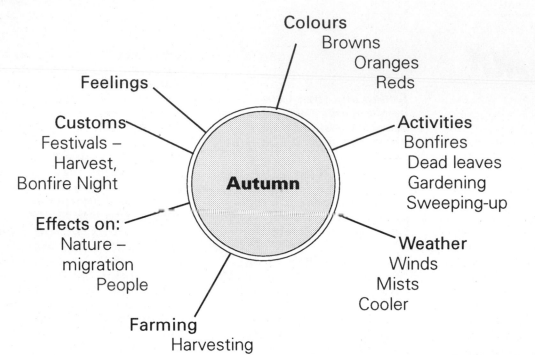

Colours
Browns
Oranges
Reds

Feelings

Customs
Festivals –
Harvest,
Bonfire Night

Autumn

Activities
Bonfires
Dead leaves
Gardening
Sweeping-up

Effects on:
Nature –
migration
People

Weather
Winds
Mists
Cooler

Farming
Harvesting

1. Autumn leaves

Age range
Five to seven.

Movement content
What – Whole body actions.
How – Quick and slow.
Where – Working on the spot
and general space.
With whom – Individuals.

Group size
Individuals.

What you need
Chosen stimulus: poetry, e.g.,
'The autumn leaves have fallen
down' (page 49); a percussion
instrument, such as a tambour.

What to do
Introduction
Ask the children to gather
around you and sit really still
while you play a rhythm on the
tambour, such as: 1,2,3,4,5,
6,7, stop. Play the rhythm
again and then ask the
children if they think they
could run away and back to
you while you play the
rhythm. Tell them to stand up
and be ready to move when
they hear the rhythm. Repeat
this idea several times and
encourage them to run into a
different space every time.
Remind them to be careful
that they do not bump into
anyone else.

Now ask them to find spaces
on their own and stand still.
Tell them that this time when

Action words

blowing	pulling	twirling	rolling	floating	twisting
turning	shaking	tugging	rising	rushing	swirling
whirling	tumbling	falling	swaying	sinking	pushing

they hear the rhythm, they are to run into another space and then stop. Again you will need to repeat this idea several times.

Movement development
Ask the children to bounce on the spot. Make sure that they are bouncing on two feet so that their heels are leaving the floor first and then their toes and encourage them to bend their knees a little to help them bounce. Tell them to stop and listen as you play a new rhythm on the tambour: 1, 2, 3 and stop. Play the rhythm two or three times so that it is quite clear to them. Ask them to, 'Bounce, bounce, bounce and stop', and travel around the room while you play the rhythm. Remind them to bend their knees and repeat this new movement phrase several times too.

Now ask the children to run, jump and roll; you can say the words as they do the actions. Repeat this several times, using the idea of blowing them around the room. Eventually tell them to stop and, where they are on the spot, slowly sink to the ground, turning or moving from side to side as they fall.

Dance idea
Ask the class to come and sit around you and to listen carefully while you read 'The autumn leaves have fallen down' or a similar poem. Discuss with them the movements they could do to the poem. Read the first verse again and ask the children to try the movements of falling, running, jumping and rolling to this verse. Read the poem as they do the movements, so that the words of the poem accompany the dance. Ask the children to make sure that

their movements take them to new spaces each time and tell them to be ready to start again immediately, so that they have plenty of time and opportunity to repeat their ideas and learn how their dances start and end. Divide the class in half and ask one half of the class to sit and watch while the other half take up their starting positions, ready to show their dances to the rest of the class. Then change over to enable the other half of the class to

share their dances while the others observe. Encourage the children who are observing to watch carefully and comment appropriately upon the dance, saying which parts they particularly liked and why.

The autumn leaves have fallen down,
Fallen down, fallen down;
The wind he came and blew them round,
And blew them around.

Let's find a brush and start to sweep,
Start to sweep, start to sweep,
And make them into a great big heap,
Into a great big heap.

Then light the bonfire and burn them away,
Burn them away, burn them away;
And now it's tidy we'll dance and play,
We'll dance and play.

Learning outcomes

In this lesson the children are involved in the interrelated processes of composing, performing and appreciating. These are the learning outcomes of this lesson and form the basis of assessment criteria linking into the Programme of Study (Common and General Requirements) and Programme of Study (Dance) in the National Curriculum.

Composing

• Select and adapt a simple phrase.
• Show a clear beginning, middle and an end.
• Experience a range of stimuli (poetry).

Performing

• Travelling, jumping and turning.

• Show an awareness of personal and general space.
• Work without interfering with others.
• Relate moving to and from the teacher.
• Respond to simple rhythms.
• Use of repetition.

Appreciating

• Observe and describe using appropriate dance vocabulary.
• Express personal preferences.
• Show sensitivity towards others when watching dance.
• Be aware of the importance of preparing the body before moving.

Follow-up ideas

A similar approach can be used to create a dance for verse two, where the leaves are swept up into a heap. Half of the class could be involved in sweeping movements, while the other half continue with the idea of the leaves

travelling and rolling, but gradually getting closer together and gathering in one particular part of the room. As they arrive close together, some should be high and some low and then continually change from high to low while turning, to show the leaves in a heap but still moving a little as the wind affects them and as other leaves arrive to add on to the heap. In verse three, ideas for flickering and leaping could be used for the burning of the bonfire, followed by the dancing and playing. This would need to be developed over several sessions.

Instead of all the class working together on every verse, divide the class up into three groups so that each group dances to one of the verses.

The life cycle of a leaf can also be explored through dance, from the shoot and growth of the leaf, swaying on the stem or branch, to the falling leaf in autumn.

Action words

swirling	dragging	rolling	bumping	spinning	turning
flying	whirling	sweeping	whisking	rustling	twisting
tumbling	falling	stirring	floating	tossing	blowing

2. Leaves blown by the wind

Age range
Seven to nine.

Movement content
What – Whole body actions and body parts.
How – Flowing, continuous.
Where – General space and levels.
With whom – Partners.

Group size
Partners.

What you need
Chosen stimulus: sound, e.g., pre-recorded wind sound effect; tape recorder; a percussion instrument, such as a tambourine.

What to do
Introduction
Ask the children each to stand still in a space on their own and tell them to listen to the sound created by you shaking the tambourine. Play the same length of rhythmical phrase two or three times so that the children know how long the sound will last. Tell them that when you play the tambourine next, you want them to travel to a different space in the room and then to travel back again to the space where they are now. Encourage them to make their movement phrase last for the same amount of time as the sound of tambourine. Then ask them to repeat their pathways, but starting from a low position and ending in a high position. Let them repeat their movement phrases several times and encourage them to think about different ways of moving from low to high and back to low so that they are ready to start again.

Movement development
Ask the children to travel around the room weaving around each other freely. As they move, encourage them to use changes in both level and speed, so that sometimes they

are moving quickly and high or slowly and low and sometimes they are moving quickly and low and then slowly and high. Repeat these ideas ensuring that the children are using their whole bodies and that they are leading their movements with different body parts; for example, leading with the hand or elbow or shoulder and so on. Introduce the use of the words 'blowing', 'whisking' and 'tossing' while the children are moving, both to stimulate and colour their movements. Repeat the words several times to enable the children to develop a different movement in response to each word.

Dance idea

First, ask the children to sit down and listen carefully to the sound effects of the wind that you have pre-recorded. Next tell them to find partners and ask each pair to stand in a space. Explain that the structure of their dances should be to start apart, meet, swirl around each other and part so that they are ready to start again. Accompany their dances with the wind sound effects and suggest that their movements should include the ideas of blowing, swirling, whisking and tossing, as well as changes in both level and speed. Remember to allow the children plenty of time to try out their ideas so that they become confident with the movements that they have selected.

Ask each pair of children to find another pair and sit near them. In their fours, they should decide which pair will dance first while the other pair observe. Ask the children to look at how the dances start, what happens in the middle and how the dances end. Then tell the pairs to change over, so that each pair has the opportunity both to dance and observe.

Learning outcomes

In this lesson the children are involved in the interrelated processes of composing, performing and appreciating. These are the learning outcomes of this lesson and form the basis of assessment criteria linking into the Programme of Study (Common and General Requirements) and Programme of Study (Dance) in the National Curriculum.

Composing
• Explore, invent, select and refine dance movements.
• Shape a simple dance with a clear structure.
• Create dances which communicate feelings, moods and ideas.
• Respond to a range of stimuli: sound.

Performing
• Isolate body parts.
• Show quality for movement.
• Make changes of level.
• Work with a partner.
• Perform and repeat simple dance phrases.
• Perform dances which communicate feelings, moods and ideas.

Appreciating
• Use appropriate vocabulary to describe dance.
• Appreciate in simple terms the aesthetic quality of dance.
• Show sensitivity when appraising others.

Follow-up ideas
To develop the performance, the class could be divided into two halves, so that one half perform their partner ideas of leaves blown by the wind and then settle, followed by the other half of the class. This will help the children to observe a variety of interpretations as well as the general effect of the dance. When they have finished, all the class could perform their dances together, to indicate that the wind has increased and all the leaves are being blown around.

3. Fireworks

Age range
Nine to eleven.

Movement content
What – Body actions.
How – Light and strong.
Where – Working on the spot and levels.
With whom – Groups.

Group size
Groups of five or six.

What you need
Chosen stimulus: poetry, e.g., 'Fireworks' by James Reeves (page 55).

What to do
Introduction
Ask the children each to stand in a space on their own and then jog or bounce gently on the spot, to ensure that their ankles and legs are warmed up. Then ask them to make themselves as small as possible, and then jump into the air making themselves as large as possible. Make sure that they land safely after jumping in the air by reminding them to bend their knees as they land. Tell them to repeat this idea several times, concentrating on making their movements explosive, sharp and strong. Let them stop so that they do not become out of breath, while you tell them that you would like them to repeat this movement but this time

Action words					
flickering	darting	fading	spinning	flying	soaring
jumping	crackling	banging	dying	spiralling	falling
rising	popping	spitting	zigzagging	shooting	bouncing
cascading	turning	exploding	roaring	leaping	fizzing

accompanying themselves with an appropriate vocal sound, for example, 'Whoosh', and trying to make 'explosive' movements in different directions.

Movement development

Now contrast these introductory ideas with the sound, 'Blip, blip. Blip, blip.' Ask the children to describe the sound. They may say that it is 'short', 'sharp' or 'jerky'. Ask them if they think that they could perform movements that have the same qualities as these words. Encourage them to perform movements that are short, sharp and jerky and to use different parts of their bodies.

In the same way, ask the children to experiment with the words 'spinning' and 'spiralling' and to accompany their movements with an appropriate vocal sound, such as, 'Wheee-e'.

Dance idea

Read a poem about Bonfire Night, such as 'Fireworks' by James Reeves, to the class. Then ask the children to get into groups of five or six. Tell them that, in their groups, they are going to create dances using the idea of a firework display as the stimulus. Encourage them to discuss in their groups the different movements that the individual fireworks suggest and the noises that they make. Let them try out some ideas and then select the ones that will be used in their display.

In order to help the groups structure their dances, ask them to think about how their firework display dance will start. How will they work together? Will they work in unison or one after the other (in canon)? How could their firework display dance end? Throughout the dance, encourage them to change levels, their individual body shapes and group shape.

Fireworks

They rise like sudden fiery flowers
    That burst upon the night,
Then fall to earth in burning showers
    Of crimson, blue, and white.

Like buds too wonderful to name,
    Each miracle unfolds,
And catherine-wheels begin to flame
    Like whirling marigolds.

Rockets and Roman candles make
    An orchard of the sky,
Whence magic trees their petals shake
    Upon each gazing eye.

James Reeves

When the class have practised and completed their dances, let each group share their dance idea for a firework display with the rest of the class. Encourage the class to describe the dances that they have observed.

Learning outcomes

In this lesson the children are involved in the interrelated processes of composing, performing and appreciating. These are the learning outcomes of this lesson and form the basis of assessment criteria linking into the Programme of Study (Common and General Requirements) and Programme of Study (Dance) in the National Curriculum.

Composing

• Explore, invent, select and refine dance movements.
• Shape a simple dance with a clear structure.
• Create dances which communicate ideas.
• Respond to a range of stimuli: poetry, sound.

Performing

• Link body actions.
• Use narrow, wide, curled, twisted, extended and contracted body shapes.
• Show quality of movement with a range of dynamics.
• Use different directions.
• Perform dances which communicate ideas.
• Make changes of level.
• Work in small groups.
• Perform and repeat simple dance phrases.

Appreciating

• Use appropriate vocabulary to describe dance.
• Show sensitivity when appraising others.
• Understand the importance of preparing the body to dance.

Follow-up ideas

After reading the poem to the class, the children could be asked to select and develop in movement two contrasting ideas and to make sounds to accompany their movements. When each group has had sufficient time to develop their dance so that they are ready to perform, the class can be asked to think about how they will perform their dance. Are all the groups going to move at the same time or will they move one group after another?

For example, each group could stand in their starting position for the display and hold this position until you, the teacher, 'light the touch paper' of one 'firework' in the group which will then start the group moving. The groups could be offset, so that eventually the whole class is involved in a giant firework display, which then gradually fizzles out.

A video or photographs may be taken of the final dance to enable the children to see the overall effect of their firework display dance.

CHAPTER 5

Winter

The topic of 'Winter' fits into other topics such as 'The seasons' and 'The weather', as well as being a topic in its own right. The inclusion of this topic In the primary curriculum offers a wealth of opportunities for work across the whole curriculum, including dance. The dance-specific topic web on page 58 shows the dance and movement possibilities that we have selected. These range from the seasonal weather of frost, snow and ice and the associated sporting activities to the excitement and build up to winter festivals such as Diwali, Hanukah and Christmas, with all its preparations, such as choosing and wrapping presents, putting up decorations and making the cake. It is the time of year when families tend to gather together to celebrate, while not forgetting the first Christmas. Our feelings at this time of the year can be very happy (as we both give and receive gifts) or, conversely, be very sad (if we are alone at this time of the year). After the New Year celebrations comes the rush of the January sales.

The three example lessons provided in this chapter all use ideas connected with snow. For the five to seven age range, a snowstorm shaker containing a model snowman is used as a visual stimulus, from which the children can take ideas of how snow falls and then of building a snowman shape. For the seven to nine age range, a poem about Jack Frost is used to stimulate ideas of scattering the silvery powder of frost around, and making sharp, spiky shapes, before melting away. 'Snow', the lesson for the nine to eleven age range, uses music as a stimulus and explores how, as the snow falls, it makes a blanket over things, creating different, rounded shapes, and how these shapes are distorted and changed as more snow falls or as the wind makes the snow drift. All of the lessons offer suggestions for follow-up work in dance.

Cross-curricular links could be developed with art, by producing snow-scene images with collage or a variety of media; with English through creative writing and poetry about snow and its effects and how the children feel when they wake up on a snowy day; with geography through locating the North and South Poles in an atlas and then discussing life in cold regions; or with science, through exploring temperature and melting and freezing.

ACTIVITIES

Feelings
Withdrawn, depressed

Effects on:
Nature – hibernation
People – clothing
Transport

Customs
Festivals –
Christmas,
Hanukah,
New Year etc.

Weather
Cold
Ice
Jack Frost
Patterns
Snow – snowman,
snowflakes,
footprints
Stillness

Winter

Colours
Sombre
Dark
White
Blues
Black

Activities
Sports – sledging,
skating, skiing
January sales

1. The Snowman

Age range
Five to seven.

Movement content
What – Moving and stillness.
How – Slow and light.
Where – Personal and general space.
With whom – Individuals.

Group size
Individuals.

What you need
Chosen stimulus: object, e.g., snowstorm shaker containing a model snowman.

What to do
Introduction
Ask the children each to find a space, away from anyone else, and then travel around the room, listening to the sound of their feet as they move. Now tell them to run around lightly, on their toes, so that they cannot hear the sound of their feet as they travel. Repeat this several times, encouraging the children to travel quietly and always to look for a space to move into, to ensure that they do not bump into anyone else.

Movement development
Ask the children to come and sit quietly on the floor all around you so that they can all see you clearly. Show them the snowstorm shaker and ask them to observe how the snowflakes move in and out, around each other and gradually fall to the bottom of the shaker. Shake it two or three times so that they can all see how the flakes fall. Ask the children to return to the spaces where they were before and see if they can move around each other as they travel lightly and then gently fall on to the ground. Remind them of how they saw the snowflakes in the shaker fall and then settle before being shaken again. Repeat the idea so that the children can clarify their movements and then ask

them to start so that they are low, near to the floor on the spot where they have been working, and to slowly rise until they are high and then return to being low. Ask them to repeat this idea but thinking about which of their body parts could lead the movement from low to high, it could be, for example, the hand, head or nose. Once they have reached as high as they can go, suggest that they can slowly 'melt,' bit by bit, until they are low again.

Dance idea
Ask the children to stand in their spaces ready to start and then begin by running in and out between each other, travelling lightly and then, gradually and gently, falling to the ground. Once they have settled near to the floor, they should begin to slowly rise from low to high. Ask them to think about the shape of the snowman that they saw in the shaker and as they rise gradually build themselves into their own snowman shape. Encourage them to decide on a definite finishing shape, for example with their hands on their hips or putting on a scarf or hat. Once they have decided on their finished shapes, suggest that they hold them, keeping very still, before slowly beginning to melt back down to the ground again. Allow the children time to practise this dance idea, in order to clarify their snowmen shapes.

When the children return to the classroom, talk about their snowmen shapes and discuss what might have made the snowmen melt. Ask them to paint pictures of their snowmen, each with a hat and scarf, before they started to melt. This will help to reinforce the snowmen shapes that they made in their dances.

Action words					
sinking	building	growing	freezing	dripping	spreading
whirling	falling	floating	settling	melting	swirling

Learning outcomes

In this lesson the children are involved in the interrelated processes of composing, performing and appreciating. These are the learning outcomes of this lesson and form the basis of assessment criteria linking into the Programme of Study (Common and General Requirements) and Programme of Study (Dance) in the National Curriculum.

Composing

• Select and adapt a simple phrase.
• Experience a range of stimuli (visual).

Performing

• Contrast between movement and stillness.
• Show an awareness of personal and general space.
• Work without interfering with others.
• Move high and low.
• Use of repetition.

Appreciating

• Show simple ways of recording dance.

Follow-up ideas

Once the children are confident of their snowmen shapes, ask half of the class to start low, ready to make their snowmen shapes, while the other half of the class travel lightly in between them. When the first snowmen shapes have melted, those children can travel lightly around the room while the others make their snowmen shapes. Other follow-up ideas might include working in pairs to build a snowman or to have a pretend snowball fight.

Action words

creeping	crunching	slipping	climbing	laughing	sliding
making	working	melting	slithering	skating	freezing
zigzagging	passing	shaking	sleeping	creating	spreading

2. Jack Frost

Age range
Seven to nine.

Movement content
What – Body parts and shapes.
How – Quick, slow and light.
Where – Pathways.
With whom – Individuals.

Group size
Individuals.

What you need
Chosen stimulus: poetry, e.g.,
'Jack Frost' by Cecily E. Pike
(page 61); tambour.

What to do
Introduction
Ask each child to stand alone
in a space and look for another
space a short distance away.
Tell the children to run as
quickly as they can to that
space when you say, 'Go'. Then
ask them to return to the
spaces where they first
started.

Tell the children to stand
still and listen as you play a
rhythm on the tambour, for
example: 1, 2, 3, 4, 1, 2, 3,
4..., emphasising the fourth
beat. Play the rhythm two or
three times so that the
children become familiar with
it and then ask them to move
away to the rhythm and then
slowly back to their starting
places. Repeat this movement
phrase several times using the
contrast of fast and slow.

Jack Frost

Look out! look out!
Jack Frost is about!
He's after your fingers and toes;
    And all through the night,
    The gay little sprite
Is working where nobody knows.

    He'll climb each tree,
    So nimble is he,
His silvery powder he'll shake;
    To windows he'll creep,
    And while we're asleep,
Such wonderful pictures he'll make.

    Across the grass,
    He'll merrily pass,
And change all its greenness to white;
Then home he will go,
And laugh, "Ho! ho! ho!
What fun I have had in the night!"

Cecily E. Pike

Movement development

Ask the children to think about all the different parts of the body that can be used to make spiky shapes, for example their fingers, knees and chins. Allow them some time to experiment with different shapes and parts of their bodies. Repeat the rhythm on the tambour and ask the children if they can now each run into a space to the rhythm and then add a spiky shape, such as sticking out their chins! Again you will need to repeat the rhythm several times so that the children can become confident of their movements. To add more variety to the spiky shapes, suggest to the children that they can make their shapes high or low, or behind or in front of their bodies. Ask some children to show their spiky shapes to the rest of the class, but ensure that those demonstrating have a variety of shapes.

Dance idea

Let the children repeat the idea of running into a space and making a spiky shape, but this time allow them to hold the spiky shape for as long as they want before running again. Remember to encourage them to move quickly and remind them that their shapes should be quick and sharp. Now ask them to select one of their spiky shapes and hold it very still; perhaps the very last spiky shape that they made. Tell them that their shapes should now begin to melt slowly and as their shapes melt they should gradually move so that, eventually, they are evenly spaced around the sides of the room.

Ask the children to gather around you and read them the poem 'Jack Frost' on page 61. Discuss the imagery used and then ask them to repeat their dances as if they were Jack Frost scattering the 'silvery powder' of frost around and, as they travel, tracing a zigzag pathway across the room. On the final spiky shape, tell the children to laugh, 'Ho! Ho! Ho!' and then to melt away and move to the side of the room saying, 'What fun I have had in the night!', just like Jack Frost in the poem.

Ask half the children to watch, while the other half of the class perform their dances. Those watching could read the poem to accompany the dances. Encourage them to observe and comment on the zigzag pathways and the spiky

shapes. Allow time in the lesson for the groups of children to change over, so that they all have an opportunity to observe and comment and then perform their dances.

Learning outcomes

In this lesson the children are involved in the interrelated processes of composing, performing and appreciating. These are the learning outcomes of this lesson and form the basis of assessment criteria linking into the Programme of Study (Common and General Requirements) and Programme of Study (Dance) in the National Curriculum.

Composing
• Explore, invent, select and refine dance movements.
• Respond to a range of stimuli: poetry.

Performing
• Use body shapes.
• Make pathways on the floor.
• Perform and repeat simple dance phrases.

Appreciating
• Use appropriate vocabulary to describe dance.
• Show sensitivity when appraising others.

Follow-up ideas
Other patterns created on a frosty day could be explored, such as first footprints. (See 'The seashore' lesson in Chapter 7 'Summer', where making footprints in the sand is discussed on page 80). Also the symmetrical shapes and patterns of snowflakes could be created by the children working in small groups.

3. Snow

Age range
Nine to eleven.

Movement content
What – Body shapes.
How – Slow and light.
Where – Levels.
With whom – Groups.

Group size
Individuals, then groups of five.

What you need
Chosen stimulus: music, e.g., *The Snowman* by Howard Blake (the soundtrack to the animated film of Raymond Briggs' story, *The Snowman*).

What to do
Introduction
Ask the children to decide if they would like to start high or low and then tell them to begin to move around the room and as they move to change levels. Introduce the word 'drifting' and ask the children to think about the qualities associated with this word as they move, so that they will show light movements and follow twisting pathways with changes of level. Repeat this several times. Remind the children that they need not move all of the time; that sometimes pauses can be included in their movement phrases.

Movement development
Ask the class to think about a movement phrase that includes the actions of 'falling', 'drifting' and 'settling'. This phrase should include changes of shape and level. Allow time for the children to explore their ideas first and, eventually, select ideas for their phrase.

Ask the children to get into groups of five, making sure that each group has their own

Action words					
swirling	skating	freezing	sinking	throwing	melting
curving	whirling	slithering	sliding	slipping	skidding
crunching	drifting	falling	floating	spinning	dripping

space. Once in their fives, ask each group to explore creating sculptured, rounded shapes that change continuously, moving at different levels. Encourage them to explore several possibilities and eventually to select three group shapes where they can move easily from one shape into the next.

Dance idea
Play the chosen music, for example part of Blake's *The Snowman*, and tell the children to listen to it. Then ask them to move away from everyone else in their group so that they are starting on their own.

Individually now, they should all repeat their phrases of falling, drifting and settling to the music three times. At the end of their third phrase, tell the members of each group to meet. They will need to decide in advance where in the room their group is going to meet. Having decided this, they can then work out where to start their own individual phrases. As this is now their starting place for the dance, ask the children to take up clear starting positions. Tell them to perform their individual phrases three times and remind them that, at the end of their third phrase, they will meet the rest of their group and form their first group shape. Ask them to continue into their other group shapes, thinking about their final group finishing position. Allow the children to repeat the dances several times so that they know exactly how the dances start, what movements they are doing in the middle and how their dances end.

Encourage each group to show their dance to the rest of the class, asking the class to observe the changing group shapes and levels. After observing each other, encourage the class to discuss the work they have seen and to describe the dances using appropriate dance vocabulary.

Learning outcomes

In this lesson the children are involved in the interrelated processes of composing, performing and appreciating. These are the learning outcomes of this lesson and form the basis of assessment criteria linking into the Programme of Study (Common and General Requirements) and Programme of Study (Dance) in the National Curriculum.

Composing

• Explore, invent, select and refine dance movements.
• Shape a simple dance with a clear structure.
• Create dances which communicate moods and ideas.
• Respond to a range of stimuli: music.

Performing

• Link body actions.
• Show quality of movement.
• Make changes of level.
• Work in small groups.
• Perform and repeat simple dance phrases.
• Perform dances which communicate moods and ideas.

Appreciating

• Use appropriate vocabulary to describe dance.
• Appreciate in simple terms the aesthetic quality of dance.
• Show sensitivity when appraising others.

Follow-up ideas

This dance idea could be developed into a snowstorm dance where the snow starts to fall and then becomes very deep, so that the shapes of everyday things become changed, and angular shapes become rounded and softened. A dramatic element could be introduced so that the mood changes. The dance could begin happily with children playing in the snow and develop to fearful, as the village is completely isolated by the bad weather or by the children being trapped in a snow drift.

CHAPTER 6

Spring

Spring is an exciting time of year when, in temperate climes, we see and experience considerable change which is distinct from the other seasons. In the dance-specific topic web for 'Spring' on page 68, we have shown how these changes can influence and stimulate ideas for dance. For example, we have selected ideas that link into: the weather including March winds and April showers, changeable weather patterns, the warmth of the sun; customs and festivals for example Easter and Saints Days such as, St David's or St Patrick's Days ; activities such as spring-cleaning and gardening; farming and the seasonal work of preparing the land, ploughing, sowing and planting; the changing colours from the dull dark colours of winter to the bright colours of spring bulbs and vivid greens; the effects on nature including the growth and life cycles of trees, plants and animals. The three lesson examples provided are based on caterpillars and butterflies, the growth of seeds and the weather. These ideas can link easily into other areas of the curriculum. All these lessons could be linked to English through using creative and descriptive vocabulary and/or listening to and responding to poetry. The caterpillars and butterflies dance idea uses contrasting movements and changing body shapes, changes in tempo and repeating rhythmic patterns, and could link with science through life cycles, with music through listening to and responding to music and to mathematics through the exploration of shapes. The growth dance idea involves the children working with partners on changing body shapes and speed. This lesson could link to work on growth and plants in science and could link with music through listening to and responding to the musical phrasing. In 'April showers', the dance idea uses a poem about a race as the stimulus for the partner dance and links well with music through composing rhythmic phrases.

ACTIVITIES

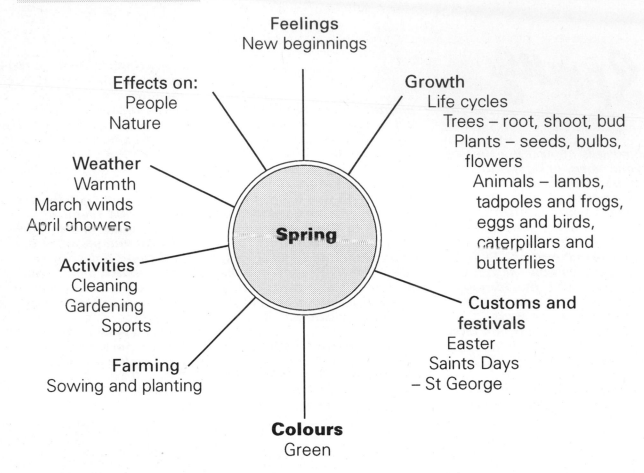

Feelings
New beginnings

Effects on:
People
Nature

Growth
Life cycles
Trees – root, shoot, bud
Plants – seeds, bulbs,
flowers
Animals – lambs,
tadpoles and frogs,
eggs and birds,
caterpillars and
butterflies

Weather
Warmth
March winds
April showers

Spring

Activities
Cleaning
Gardening
Sports

Customs and
festivals
Easter
Saints Days
– St George

Farming
Sowing and planting

Colours
Green

1. Caterpillars and butterflies

Age range
Five to seven.

Movement content
What – Body parts.
How – Quick and slow.
Where – General space and levels.
With whom – Individuals.

Group size
Individuals.

What you need
Chosen stimulus: poetry, e.g., 'Caterpillars only crawl' by S. and P. Charlton (see page 69); tambour or drum.

What to do
Introduction
Ask the children to walk around the room, weaving in and out of each other without touching. Now ask them to make their steps as big and slow as they can. Tell the children to listen to you making a slow, strong sound on the tambour. Can they now repeat their big, slow steps to the accompaniment of the tambour? When they hear the sound of the tambour change to a quick light sound, they should change from making large, slow steps to making small, quick, light steps. Try this several times to allow the children to practise changing from slow steps to quick steps according to the tambour accompaniment.

Movement development

Using the tambour, play a $^4/_4$ rhythm (1,2,3,4...) several times and ask the children to listen to it. Then ask them to try to walk and then crawl to the rhythm, using four bars of $^4/_4$. Tell the children to stop and nod their heads from side to side to the rhythm too.

Ask the children each to move into a space and curl up very small, like a ball, and then stretch out along the floor. Can they make their bodies as long and thin as possible, as a contrast to the curled shape? Finally, encourage the children to combine these two ideas so that they curl up and stretch out, and curl up and stretch out and so on as they travel along the floor, using four bars of $^4/_4$.

Dance idea

Read the poem to the children.
Ask them to space themselves around the room. Can they now travel in and out around each other lightly, on their toes, to the first four lines of the poem (or to a

Caterpillars only crawl

A butterfly was flying by a garden in July;
He landed on a cabbage leaf and heard a mournful sigh. (Sigh.)
A big, fat, hairy caterpillar, nibbling at a leaf,
Said, 'If I could fly like you, that would be a relief.

But, caterpillars only crawl, caterpillars only crawl,
Crawling here, nibbling there, crawling and nibbling everywhere
Caterpillars only crawl and though I'd like to reach the garden wall,
On this leaf I'll stay, nibbling away, never getting anywhere at all.'

'Now, look here', said the butterfly. 'Not very long ago,
I sat and nibbled leaves like you and moved around so slow.
But soon you'll be a butterfly, and through the leaves you'll flutter by,
And you will be so happy that you never more will say...

Caterpillars only crawl, caterpillars only crawl
Crawling here, nibbling there, crawling and nibbling everywhere
Caterpillars only crawl, well, crawl and nibble that's all,
But one fine day, you'll fly away and flutter by the garden wall.'

Sue and Peter Charlton

Action words					
crawling	creeping	curling	stretching	flying	fluttering
flitting	settling	hovering	munching	landing	nibbling

tambour)? When they stop, ask them to finish in a low shape near the floor. Let the children practise their ideas to the music so that they begin to understand when to begin and when to finish their movement phrases.

Now ask the children to listen to this rhythmic phrase: 'Crawl, 2, 3, stop; crawl, 2, 3, stop; nod, 2, 3, stop; nod, 2, 3, stop'. Can they move to it? Repeat this phrase several times to let them clarify their movements, crawling near to the ground, nodding their heads and moving to the rhythm. Put these ideas together and ask the children to start from the beginning; travelling around the room between each other, lightly on their toes, and ending up near the floor and then crawling and nodding to the second verse of the poem. Ask the children if they can remember how they curled up small and stretched out along the floor, like the movements of a caterpillar, and see if they can now perform this movement phrase, of curling up and stretching out, to the third verse. Finally for the fourth verse, ask the children to repeat the crawling and nodding phrase, travelling to the centre of the room to gather around you, finishing their dance by stretching up tall.

Ask half the class to sit down and observe the other half of the class perform the dance. Encourage the children each to watch one person in the dance and give them something specific to look for; for example, 'Does your chosen person's dance show a clear beginning, middle and end?' or 'Does his or her dance show a contrast of quick and slow movements?'

These ideas may take several sessions to complete; for example, in session one the children could experience and develop the travelling in and out and crawling phrases. In the second session, they could develop the curling and stretching idea and, finally, in the third session they could revise their dance phrases and put them together to perform the dance to the poem or they could use percussion instruments to accompany their dance.

Learning outcomes

In this lesson the children are involved in the interrelated processes of composing, performing and appreciating. These are the learning outcomes of this lesson and form the basis of assessment criteria linking into the Programme of Study (Common and General Requirements) and Programme of Study (Dance) in the National Curriculum.

Composing
• Invent a simple phrase.
• Show a clear beginning, middle and an end.

Performing
• Travelling.
• Contrast between movement and stillness.
• Show an awareness of general space.
• Respond to simple rhythms.

Appreciating
• Show sensitivity towards others when watching dance.

Follow-up ideas

Read the story of *The Very Hungry Caterpillar* by Eric Carle (1970, Hamish Hamilton) to the children and develop movement ideas from the text. This story follows the life cycle of a butterfly. Similar ideas could be developed on the life cycle of a frog from spawn to tadpole to adult frog, or the life cycle of a bird from egg to chick to fledged bird.

and dodge and turn while running and ask them to try crouching and stretching out in different directions; upwards, outwards, behind and so on. Let the children move to the rhythm of the words and practise crouching and stretching out on the spot and then running to another space to crouch and stretch.

Movement development
Ask the children to curl up tightly near to the floor and slowly stretch their whole bodies out into the space around them. Let them repeat this movement several times, starting on different parts of the body; for example from their knees, backs, feet, sides and so on. Ask them to curl up and, to a count of eight, stretch out using a different body part (such as a hand, a shoulder or an elbow) to lead the way, pushing upwards and outwards. Ensure that the stretching movement lasts the whole eight counts. Give the children time to practise their movements.

Dance idea
Discuss with the class the cycle of growth from seed to plant and ask the children to suggest words to describe this process. Offer some of the action words at the beginning of this lesson if they need ideas to start them off. Tell the class how they can make up a partner dance using the idea of growth, giving them the following (or a similar)

2. Seeds and growth

Age range
Seven to nine.

Movement content
What – Body parts and body shapes.
How – Quick and slow, light and strong.
Where – Personal and general space.
With whom – Partners.

Group size
Partners.

What you need
Chosen stimuli: action words, e.g., words relating to the growth of plants; tape recorder.

What to do
Introduction
Ask the children to listen to this phrase, 'Crouch and spread, crouch and spread, run, run, run, run, crouch and spread.' Now see if they can crouch down and stretch out wide on the floor on their backs, then their stomachs and then their feet.

Now ask the children to move to the phrase, 'Crouch and spread...'. Repeat the phrase several times, encouraging the class to weave

Action words					
rising	unfolding	stretching	curling	bending	swaying
pushing	falling	crouching	spreading	twisting	turning
reaching	spiralling	contorting	bursting	thrusting	growing
uncurling	awakening	blossoming	opening	clinging	sinking

framework. Ask each child to find a partner, one to be 'A' and the other to be 'B'. A should curl up near the floor and remain still, while B travels around the room, weaving, dodging and turning, before returning to her partner and finishing by spreading, curling and surrounding A. Ask A to uncurl for eight counts while B remains still. Ask them to repeat this idea to help them understand the phrasing of the movement.

Next ask B to uncurl for eight counts while A remains still and then A to uncurl for eight counts while B remains still. Ask the children to go back to the beginning and see if they can now perform all of their movements to the music.

The speed of the movement now changes, so ask the children if they can try to move more quickly too. Tell A to make a shape for two counts followed by B making a shape for two counts, then A again and finally B. Repeat this movement idea to encourage the children to move quickly and make clear body shapes. Now go back to the very beginning and put all their movement ideas together with the music.

When they have practised their dances several times, ask each pair to show their choreography to another pair. Encourage each group of four to discuss what they have seen and help each other to improve their dances; for example, suggest that they think about body shape. Are they using all the music? Are they using a variety of body parts to lead their movements?

If the suggested music is unavailable, you could develop the use of action words as a starting point.

Learning outcomes

In this lesson the children are involved in the interrelated processes of composing, performing and appreciating. These are the learning outcomes of this lesson and form the basis of assessment criteria linking into the Programme of Study (Common and General Requirements) and Programme of Study (Dance) in the National Curriculum.

Composing
• Explore, invent, select and refine dance movements.
• Shape a simple dance.
• Respond to a range of stimuli: action words.

Performing
• Link body actions.
• Isolate body parts.
• Use wide and curled body shapes.
• Work with a partner.

Appreciating
• Use appropriate vocabulary to describe dance.
• Show sensitivity when appraising others.

Follow-up ideas

The children could take several lessons to complete their dance using the idea of growth. Give the class plenty of time to practise and perfect their ideas before sharing their dances with others. You may want to continue the idea of growth by developing the idea of change; change in shape and form, from small to large, or change from baby to child, to adolescent, to adulthood, to old age.

Action words

pitter-patter	beating	flowing	splashing	streaming
pelting	raining	oozing	rushing	trickling
dropping	running	racing	winning	dripping

3. April showers

Age range
Nine to eleven.

Movement content
What – Travelling and stillness.
How – Quick and slow.
Where – Directions.
With whom – Partners.

Group size
Partners.

What you need
Chosen stimulus: poetry, e.g.,
'Waiting at the window' by
A. A. Milne (photocopiable
page 179).

What to do
Introduction
Ask the class to clap their
hands on the floor starting
slowly and getting quicker and
quicker. Let them practise
increasing the speed. Now ask
them to clap their hands
against different parts of their
bodies, such as their legs,
arms, chests, thighs and so on.
Next tell them to stamp their
feet on the spot, starting
slowly and getting quicker and
quicker. Can they stamp their
feet while travelling all around
the room and, at the same
time, add changes of direction,
for example stamping
forwards, backwards or
sideways?

As a contrast, ask the class
to repeat these ideas but
changing the dynamics of the
movements, for example using
light and quick steps, gentle
claps and using the word

'pattering' as a stimulus to
achieve the appropriate
movement quality.

Movement development
Ask the children to choose
partners and together create
rhythmic movement phrases
with their hands and feet,
using the floor and different
parts of their bodies.

In their pairs, ask them to
begin away from each other
and, using their rhythmic
phrases, travel towards and
around each other. Let them
experiment with these ideas,
including a change in level and
trying to do the opposite to
their partners; for example, if
one person is clapping her
hands high, then the other
may be clapping his hands
low.

Waiting at the window

These are my two drops of rain
Waiting at the window pane.

I am waiting here to see
Which the winning one will be.

Both of them have different names.
One is John and one is James.

All the best and all the worst
Comes from which of them is first.

James has just begun to ooze.
He's the one I want to lose.

John is waiting to begin.
He's the one I want to win.

James is going slowly on.
Something sort of sticks to John.

John is moving off at last.
James is going pretty fast.

John is rushing down the pane.
James is going slow again.

James has met a sort of smear.
John is getting very near.

Is he going fast enough?
(James has found a piece of fluff.)

John has hurried quickly by.
(James was talking to a fly.)

John is there, John has won!
Look! I told you! Here's the sun!

A.A. Milne

Dance idea

Give the children copies of the poem 'Waiting at the window', (photocopiable page 179). In their pairs, ask the children to compose a dance using the idea of a race, as in the poem. Tell them to start side by side, as they would do at the beginning of the race. Using the movement phrases they have been working on during the lesson, ask them to choreograph dances which include forwards and backwards directions and changes of speed and level. Encourage them to vary the number of steps they take in each direction. As the dance begins to take shape, ask them to identify where their dances will start and finish. At this stage, tell each pair to join up with another pair and share the dances they have composed so far. Encourage them to observe each other and make useful suggestions to help clarify the movements. Give the children adequate time to experiment and select ideas. Demand finished dances that have clear structures and quality before letting the children share their dances with each other.

Learning outcomes

In this lesson the children are involved in the interrelated processes of composing, performing and appreciating. These are the learning outcomes of this lesson and form the basis of assessment criteria linking into the Programme of Study (Common and General Requirements) and Programme of Study (Dance) in the National Curriculum.

Composing

• Explore, invent, select and refine dance movements.
• Shape a simple dance with a clear structure.
• Respond to a range of stimuli: poetry.

Performing

• Show quality of movement with a range of dynamics.
• Use different directions.
• Make changes of level.
• Work with a partner.

Appreciating

• Use appropriate vocabulary to describe dance.
• Show sensitivity when appraising others.

Follow-up ideas

When the children have finished their dances, ask them if they want to perform their dances in silence, to the poem being read out aloud by one person or by several people or to part of the poem. How will they adapt their dances to their chosen accompaniment?

Give the children the opportunity to respond to a wide range of stimuli. For example, their dances could be performed to a tape recording, used as a background sound, of the rain beating down on the pavement or against the window pane.

Use the video of the song 'Singing in the rain', being danced and sung by Gene Kelly in the film of the same name, as a starting point for individual or partner work. Umbrellas could be used as props for the dance; explore the opening and closing of the umbrella, huddling underneath an umbrella individually and in groups and moving with the umbrella, hiding behind it and so on. The thunderstorm itself could be used as an environmental stimulus. Consider the movements and range of dynamics associated with thunder and lightning.

Develop the race idea into a dance based on an athletic activity, beginning with a sprint start, then the running and then the finish, with breaking the tape. For example, in threes, the children could choreograph a dance in slow motion where one dancer makes a sprint start and is joined by the second dancer running, and they are joined by the third dancer racing for the finishing line.

CHAPTER 7

Summer

'The weather' and 'The cycle of the seasons' are used regularly for topic work in the primary school at various times of the year. In this chapter we have focused on 'Summer'. From the overall topic of 'The weather' a dance-specific topic web has been devised which identifies the possibilities for dance (see page 78). These could link into explorations of: hot summer weather, shadows and thunderstorms; nature, growth and cycles; customs and festivals such as May Day, maypole and morris dancing, rain dances, summer fairs and holidays.

The three lesson examples are based on the seashore, shadows and sea creatures. 'The seashore' dance idea uses air and floor patterns, which could link with maths through repeating patterns, with music through listening to phrases, with geography through maps and routes and with art through printing and mark-making. 'The shadow' dance idea links with language through using poetry and imagery, with maths through shapes, symmetry and asymmetry and matching, and with science through exploring and making shadows. The 'Sea creatures' dance idea uses action words to describe movements which links obviously with work on descriptive language. This lesson could also be linked into music through developing rhythmical phrases using the voice or percussion instruments, with science through studying life under the sea, and with art through making imaginative drawings, collages or sculptures.

ACTIVITIES

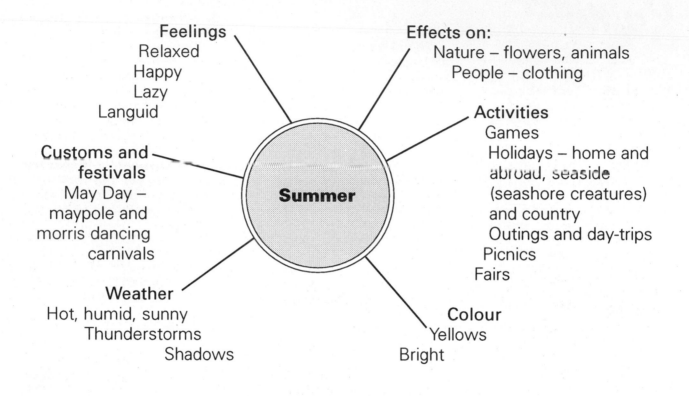

Feelings
Relaxed
Happy
Lazy
Languid

Effects on:
Nature – flowers, animals
People – clothing

Customs and festivals
May Day –
maypole and
morris dancing
carnivals

Summer

Activities
Games
Holidays – home and
abroad, seaside
(seashore creatures)
and country
Outings and day-trips
Picnics
Fairs

Weather
Hot, humid, sunny
Thunderstorms
Shadows

Colour
Yellows
Bright

1. The seashore

Age range
Five to seven.

Movement content
What – Whole body actions.
How – Straight and roundabout.
Where – Patterns and pathways.
With whom – Individuals.

Group size
Individuals.

What you need
Chosen stimulus: music, e.g., 'Orinoco Flow' on Watermark by Enya (Warner), 'Summer song' by C. Benstead on *Music for Dance (Tape III)* (Music for Dance, PO Box 727, London, SE18 3DX) or 'I do like to be beside the seaside' by J. A. Glover-Kind in *Ta-ra-ra boom-de-ay: Songs for everyone* chosen by D. Gadsby and B. Harrop (1977, A&C Black); tape recorder; photocopiable page 180.

What to do
Introduction
Give each child a copy of photocopiable page 180 and ask them to look at the different patterns. Tell them to select one of the patterns and draw it in the air several times using their forefingers or whole hands, making the patterns big, clear and slow. Make sure the children use both hands alternately so that their arms do not tire and so

that they have the experience of moving both arms and both hands. Encourage them to really bend and stretch; sometimes reaching high, sometimes bending low and sometimes stretching from side to side as they each draw their pattern in the air. Now ask them to repeat their patterns in the air but making them as big as possible by starting at one end of the room and finishing at the other end. Remind them to avoid bumping into each other as they move around the room. Now see if they can join the two movements together; drawing their patterns in the air on the spot and then to fill the whole room.

Movement development
Ask the children each to repeat the pathway that they have just travelled along, but this time sometimes going forwards and sometimes going backwards, while continuing to make their patterns in the air. Ask them to think about different ways of travelling along their pathways – can they hop, jump, turn, slide and so on?

Dance idea
Play the music chosen as the stimulus and tell the children to listen carefully to it. Ask them if they think they could draw their patterns in the air, on the spot and around the room to it. Play the music several times and let the children try their movements, giving them opportunities to practise their ideas. Encourage

them to review their ideas – do their pathways need changing in any way, perhaps to avoid bumping into someone? Ask them to go back to the spaces where they started and repeat their dances. Remind them to consider where their dances will finish.

When the children return to the classroom, talk to them about the patterns and pathways they performed in their dance lesson. Ask them each to try and draw the pattern they made on the floor on the photocopiable page. This reinforces the learning that took place during the lesson by helping the children to visualise and clarify the patterns and pathways they made. The pages will also form a record of evidence for the teacher to keep as an example of a simple way of recording dance and to see if individual children understand and can visualise patterns and pathways.

Action words

blazing	melting	drying	sunbathing	lazing	dozing
relaxing	sleeping	yawning	buzzing	stinging	running
playing	bouncing	catching	throwing	chopping	kicking
digging	building	burying	sailing	boating	snorkelling
fishing	flying	spinning	swimming	splashing	paddling
floating	tapping	flowing	rushing	rippling	crashing
rolling	trickling	drinking	swirling	swishing	surfing

Learning outcomes

In this lesson the children are involved in the interrelated processes of composing, performing and appreciating. These are the learning outcomes of this lesson and form the basis of assessment criteria linking into the Programme of Study (Common and General Requirements) and Programme of Study (Dance) in the National Curriculum.

Composing

• Select and adapt a simple phrase.

Performing

• Contrast between movement and stillness.
• Contrast between large and small shapes.
• Move forwards, backwards and sideways.
• Work without interfering with others.
• Use of repetition.

Appreciating

• Show simple ways of recording dance.

Follow-up ideas

During the introduction to the lesson, let the children experience drawing a variety of patterns in the air using their fingers and hands, for example spirals, zigzags, curved and straight lines, circles, figures of eight and combinations of straight and curved lines. Encourage them to use other parts of their bodies with which to draw their patterns such as their wrists, elbows, shoulders, noses, chins or knees.

When the children move on to making their patterns on the floor, tell them to imagine using their feet to make footprints in the sand. How do they make their footprints – heels first, on tiptoe, with the outsides or insides of their feet?

Encourage the children to make up their own patterns and pathways not given on the photocopiable page. Perhaps they could they write their initials, their ages or their names in the air and/or on the floor. This idea can be developed by using different body parts and making the movements fast, slow, big, small, on the spot and so on.

Once they are confident of their dances individually, ask each child to find a partner. In their pairs, ask them to show their partners their patterns – can each child describe his own and his partner's pattern? Then suggest that in each pair the children try to copy each other's patterns and pathways.

Action words					
following	copying	shadowing	tracing	matching	imitating
spreading	curling	changing	stretching	rushing	racing
jumping	creeping	curving	turning	elongating	shrinking

2. The shadow

Age range
Seven to nine.

Movement content
What – Whole body actions.
How – Quick and slow.
Where – General space and levels.
With whom – Partners, leader and follower, and shadowing.

Group size
Partners.

What you need
Chosen stimulus: poetry, e.g., 'The Shadow' by Edith M. Stokes (page 82); photocopiable page 181.

What to do
Introduction
Ask the children to find partners and travel around the room together, one behind the other, walking, hopping and skipping as they go. While they are travelling, ask them to change their speed. Can they now repeat some of these ways of travelling, but trying to take big steps and then small steps? Suggest that they see if the leaders can catch their partners out by suddenly changing the size and speed of their steps. Change over the leaders regularly so that both partners can have a turn at leading.

Movement development
Ask the class to tell you the kinds of shapes their bodies can make; for example stretched and wide, stretched and thin, tucked and rounded or twisted. Then ask the children to decide, in their pairs, who is going to be 'A' and who will be 'B'. A should then make any body shape, which B can copy. A then makes a different body shape for B to copy. Now B chooses any shape for A to copy and then makes another shape for A to copy. Encourage the children to try many different body shapes. Ask them to make up their own movement phrases where A begins stretched flat and wide and then curls up, like a ball, stretches long and thin and finally makes a twisted shape.

The shadow

On sunny days I am never free,
For I have a friend who comes with me.
He says no word, he makes no sound,
Yet I know well that he will be found
On the ground or up the wall,
Spread and flat or twelve feet tall.

I curl myself up like a ball:
He changes too, to very small.
I stretch right out, all long and thin,
And there he is, just like a pin.
I make myself feel like a screw,
But now, of course, he will do it too.

I rush along with huge great paces,
But he comes too – in fact, he races.
I test him out, and go so slow.
Confound the fellow! Why won't he go?
To catch him out, I jump up high.
At last I've got him. He can't fly.

Edith M. Stokes

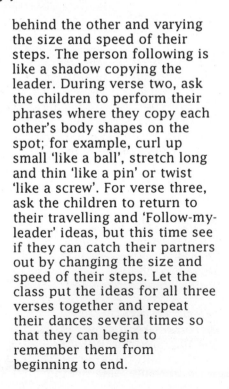

Each time A changes body shape B should try to copy the new shape. Encourage the children to make clear shapes and to use different levels throughout their phrases. Change over who is A and who is B regularly so that B has the opportunity to lead the movement.

Dance idea
Read aloud a suitable poem, such as 'The Shadow' by Edith M. Stokes. Then ask the class to tell you about the shapes made by the shadow in the poem. You may need to read the poem again to clarify this discussion. The poem could be used to accompany the dance, so that the children are moving while the poem is being read out, or the poem can be used just to help the children structure their dances.

To verse one, the children can use their ideas of travelling around the room and following their partners, one behind the other and varying the size and speed of their steps. The person following is like a shadow copying the leader. During verse two, ask the children to perform their phrases where they copy each other's body shapes on the spot; for example, curl up small 'like a ball', stretch long and thin 'like a pin' or twist 'like a screw'. For verse three, ask the children to return to their travelling and 'Follow-my-leader' ideas, but this time see if they can catch their partners out by changing the size and speed of their steps. Let the class put the ideas for all three verses together and repeat their dances several times so that they can begin to remember them from beginning to end.

Ask each pair to join with another. In their fours, give one of the pairs a copy of photocopiable page 181. The other pair can then perform their dance, while the first pair observe the dance and select the body shapes on the photocopiable page that they see the performers make. Tell the pairs to change over and let the observers perform their dances. Now ask the children to discuss and describe with their partners what they saw. Did they see all four body shapes and were the shapes clear? Encourage the children to help each other, where necessary, to improve their dances.

Giving them the opportunity to observe, identify body shapes and describe and discuss their dances with their partners will help the children to clarify and understand their own body shapes in their dances. This photocopiable page can be used, therefore, for pupil self-assessment and as a record of evidence.

This dance idea may take several lessons to complete and would make a unit of work. During session one the children could work on 'Follow-my-leader' and developing their movement

ideas to the first verse of the poem. In session two they could move on to making up a movement phrase, copying body shapes as in verse two. In the third session, the class could work in pairs on the 'Follow-my-leader' idea, trying to catch their partners out. Finally, in the last session, they could put all these ideas together to make their shadow dances.

Learning outcomes

In this lesson the children are involved in the interrelated processes of composing, performing and appreciating. These are the learning outcomes of this lesson and form the basis of assessment criteria linking into the Programme of Study (Common and General Requirements) and Programme of Study (Dance) in the National Curriculum.

Composing
• Shape a simple dance with a clear structure.
• Respond to a range of stimuli: poetry.

Performing
• Link body actions.
• Use narrow, wide, curled and twisted body shapes.
• Make changes in levels.
• Show a range of dynamics.
• Work with a partner (following and copying).

Appreciating
• Use appropriate vocabulary to describe dance.
• Show different ways of recording dance.

Follow-up ideas
The children's body shapes can be developed by mirroring (copying a partner as a reflection, slowly changing shape); for example, as in the 'Hall of mirrors'. Ask the children to see if they can do the opposite to their partners so, for example, when one child is stretching high, the other should be bent low, or when one child is stretched, the other should be curled. Ask the children, when working individually, to change from one body shape to another by adding a turn or a jump.

3. Sea creatures

Age range
Nine to eleven.

Movement content
What – Whole body actions.
How – Quick and slow.
Where – Levels and directions.
With whom – Individuals and groups.

Group size
Individuals, then groups of five.

What you need
Chosen stimuli: action words, e.g., words describing the movement of sea creatures, and music, e.g., 'The octopus' garden' on *Abbey Road* by The Beatles (Apple Records) or *Waiting for Cousteau* by J.M. Jarre (Polydor); tape recorder; photocopiable page 182.

What to do
Introduction
Ask the children to reach upwards as high as they can. Make sure that they are really stretching. Encourage them to reach in other directions: sideways, backwards, high and low, sometimes reaching quickly and sometimes slowly, bringing their arms back towards the mid-line of their bodies each time.

Movement development
Using the words 'reaching', 'trapping' and 'withdrawing', in any order they like, ask the children to create a movement phrase. Tell them to repeat the phrase several times so that a rhythm is developed; for example, 'Withdraw, withdraw, reach, reach, trap.'

Dance idea
Ask the children to work in groups of five and think about a fantasy sea creature and how it might move. Tell them to choose three words to describe their sea creature's movement. The list of action words at the bottom of this page describing how sea creatures can move may help them. They should try now to create a rhythmical phrase using the words they have chosen, thinking about how and where their sea creature will move. What shape is their sea creature? How will this affect the way they move? When the groups have had sufficient time to select, practise and perfect their dances let the whole class watch each group perform their dance. While they watch, see if the rest of the class can find words to describe the sea creature being represented.

When the children get back to the classroom ask them to write down on the photocopiable page provided (page 182) the three words that they selected to describe how their sea creature moved.

Action words

| scuttling | scurrying | wriggling | slithering | sliding | reaching |
| grasping | trapping | withdrawing | darting | gliding | waving |

Underneath the words they can try to draw their fantasy sea creature. This worksheet is valuable for self-evaluation, to reinforce the learning outcomes of the lesson and as a record of evidence for teacher assessment.

Learning outcomes
In this lesson the children are involved in the interrelated processes of composing, performing and appreciating. These are the learning outcomes of this lesson and form the basis of assessment criteria linking into the Programme of Study (Common and General Requirements) and Programme of Study (Dance) in the National Curriculum.

Composing
• Explore, invent, select and refine dance movements.
• Respond to a range of stimuli: action words.

Performing
• Link body actions.
• Use extended and contracted body shapes.
• Use different directions.
• Make changes of level.
• Show a range of dynamics.
• Perform a variety of rhythms.
• Perform and repeat a simple dance.
• Work in small groups.

Appreciating
• Use appropriate vocabulary to describe dance.
• Show different ways of recording dance.

Follow-up ideas
Play the suggested music and let the children listen to it. Use the music as background sound and let the class perform their sea creature dances over it. Ask the groups to get into their starting positions and let them begin their dances one after the other, so that one group starts followed by the next group and so on until the whole class are moving (this is called 'moving in canon'). Some groups will finish before others because each individual group dance will be of a different length, so encourage them to hold their last group shape until the whole class are still.

See also the dance idea in Chapter 11, 'Water', 'Under the sea' on page 119.

CHAPTER 8

Earth

'Earth' is a topic which enables teachers to consider many areas within science and geography. In science this involves two of the National Curriculum attainment targets: 'Life and living processes' (AT2) and 'Materials and their properties' (AT3). In geography the two attainment targets involved are: 'Knowledge and understanding of places' (AT2) and 'Environmental geography' (AT5) through which this topic also relates directly to the Scottish guidelines.

The dance-specific topic web for 'Earth' on page 88, shows many different movement possibilities through which dance can be linked into these curriculum areas. The topic web considers: the physical environment, its land-forms and changing landscapes; structures, life and work underground; exploration over land and sea; the colours and feelings the earth suggests; conservation and pollution; and the effects of farming, the seasons, the climate and natural 'disasters' such as earthquakes on the land.

The three example lessons in this chapter are based on minibeasts, pollution and the physical environment.

'Minibeasts' is used regularly as a topic in its own right at Key Stage 1. The 'Minibeasts' dance lesson considers through movement the shape and size and variety of these creatures living underground and the different ways in which they move. This links well with science in the 'variety of living things' aspect of 'Life and living processes'. The lesson on pollution focuses on the quality of the environment by exploring the idea of litter, a subject regularly discussed with children. The dance idea is to create a heap of decomposing litter and to think about the shapes of different items of litter before and after they have been thrown away. The third lesson considers land-forms and changing landscapes through creating group dances. The contrast between the soft contours of the downs and the rugged, rocky, mountain peaks is shown by changing the groups' shapes, line and form using a variety of levels and a range of dynamics.

ACTIVITIES

Feelings
Security, stability

Underground
Soil
Passages and tunnels
Creatures – minibeasts,
worm casts
Mining – metals,
diamonds
Pollution
Noise, traffic
Water
Sewage, litter,
rubbish Ozone
Effects on the land
Farming
Seasons
Climate
Tremors
Earthquakes
Volcanoes

Earth

Physical environment
Industry
Buildings
Skyline
Land-forms – mountains,
valleys and plains, hills and
downs, rocks and cliffs
Exploration
Land
Jungles and deserts
Polar regions
Sea
Colours
Black
Brown
Green
Conservation
Waste, recycling
Wildlife – plants, rainforests

1. Minibeasts

Age range
Five to seven.

Movement content
What – Whole body actions.
How – Quick and slow.
Where – Personal and general
space, directions.
With whom – Individuals.

Group size
Individuals.

What you need
Chosen stimulus:
environmental, e.g., live
minibeasts, and visual, e.g.,
pictures of minibeasts.

What to do
Introduction
Take the children outside and
encourage them to look for
minibeasts. Where will they

find them? Lift up a paving
slab or a stone or an old
piece of wood and look out
for beetles 'scurrying', ants
'rushing', woodlice 'curling',
worms 'wriggling', spiders
'running', snails 'creeping',
or slugs 'slithering'. Ask the
children to observe the way
the minibeasts move and
their shapes and sizes.
   Back in the hall or
classroom, ask the children
to run everywhere round the
room. Tell them to think
about 'rushing' this way and
that, 'being busy', and 'never
stopping'.

Movement development

As a contrast to the rushing movement, ask the children to curl up and, using their hands and knees, creep and crawl at 'a snail's pace', slowly moving along the floor. Let the children practice moving slowly as they will find this very difficult at first. Now see if they can move slowly with another part of their bodies touching the floor, first moving forwards and then backwards. Ask the children to put these two movements together, starting by crawling on their hands and knees and then on another part of their bodies.

Show the children some pictures of minibeasts. Ask them to try to move like one of the creatures. Remind them to think about the shape and speed of their chosen creature. Is it big or small and does it move quickly or slowly?

Dance idea

Talk to the class about the minibeasts they have seen outside and in the pictures and about the movements they have been doing in the dance lesson. Ask them to find a starting place in the hall and begin by rushing everywhere, making quick, light steps. They should then change to moving slowly on their hands and knees along the floor and then on another part of their bodies. To finish their dances, see if the children can remember how to move like the creatures they chose. Eventually, ask the children to go back to the spaces where they started and perform the three ideas again together. Divide the class in half and let one half of the class at a time perform their dances while the other half watch. Encourage the children to sit quietly and observe the different ways the children move, noting when they move quickly and when they move slowly.

Action words					
exploring	over	under	round	through	creeping
scurrying	rushing	running	burrowing	burying	slithering
sliding	wriggling	curling	stopping	sleeping	around

Learning outcomes

In this lesson the children are involved in the interrelated processes of composing, performing and appreciating. These are the learning outcomes of this lesson and form the basis of assessment criteria linking into the Programme of Study (Common and General Requirements) and Programme of Study (Dance) in the National Curriculum.

Composing
• Invent and select a simple phrase.
• Show a clear beginning, middle and end.

Performing
• Travelling.
• Contrast between movement and stillness.
• Demonstrate the difference between fast and slow movements.
• Move forwards and backwards.
• Perform a simple phrase.

Appreciating
• Show sensitivity towards others when watching dance.

Follow-up ideas

This dance idea can be developed by looking at other minibeasts and animals which live underground. Let the children explore the changing shapes and ways of moving of, for example, spiders: curling up very small, weaving in and out, dangling and swinging to and fro, spinning, running and stopping, catching and trapping. Then let them choose two or three of these movements and put them together, encouraging them to change their body shapes and the speed of their movements. Alternatively, let the children investigate the movements of a colony of ants: worker ants, soldier ants and flying ants.

Ask the children to design a pathway or route that a mole or rabbit might make underground: burrowing and tunnelling, undulating up and down. When the children have made up their routes see if they can move forwards and backwards along these pathways changing levels as they go, sometimes moving on their hands and feet and sometimes moving on other parts of their bodies.

Action words

| denting | squeezing | collapsing | crumpling | contracting | blowing |
| expanding | popping | shaking | scrunching | dropping | rotting |

...Litter appeared on the streets again. Empty cans, greasy fish and chip wrappings, old newspapers and broken glass bottles once again lay in festering heaps by the side of the road.

...So the piles of litter just grew bigger. In six weeks city centres throughout the land were overshadowed by vast amounts of plastic food cartons and scrunched up sweet papers. Waves of soggy cardboard boxes, mouldy food and rotting shoes sloshed out of the cities into the countryside, and it was not long before a National Emergency was announced. Great Britain was being buried under a top soil of stinking rubbish.

2. Pollution

Age range
Seven to nine

Movement content
What – Body shapes.
How – Quick and slow.
Where – General space and levels.
With whom – Small groups and whole class.

Group size
In groups of three, then whole class.

What you need
Chosen stimuli: objects, e.g., a clean empty soft-drink can and an empty crisp packet, and literature, e.g., extract from 'The litter bug' in *Grizzly Tales for Gruesome Kids* by J. Rix (see above).

What to do
Introduction
Show the children an empty soft-drink can and then squeeze it, to collapse it and crumple it up. Ask the children each to make a large body shape and then make a crumpled body shape. Ask them to try this idea again, but this time moving one part of the body at a time, just like dents being put in the can.

Encourage the children to make three quick movements one after the other before 'collapsing', 'scrunching' and 'crumpling'. Discuss with the class how and where you would throw away the squashed can; for example tossing it in a bin, kicking it in the gutter or throwing it over your shoulder. Are all these alternatives environmentally acceptable? Now let the children try some of these ideas in movement. Can they put the ideas of collapsing and throwing together. Let them now try jumping and turning before landing in a heap too.

Movement development
Show the class an empty crisp packet. Blow up the empty bag and burst it. Using the idea of gradually expanding and then bursting, ask the children to

make a small body shape, gradually making it bigger and then making an explosive movement. Ask the children each to think of other bits of rubbish, that they regularly throw away, that could be a starting point for movement. For example, a plastic ketchup bottle might suggest shaking and squeezing movements, vegetable peelings might suggest spiralling, and opening and closing movements might be stimulated by a hinged polystyrene burger carton. Ask the class to individually choose one piece of rubbish and see if they can put the movements it suggests into a phrase; based, for example, on: 'Scrunch it up and throw it away to land on the rubbish heap'.

Dance idea
Ask the children to get into groups of three. Let each group choose three different pieces of rubbish and discuss their movement phrases and how they will work together. Ask them to think about where and how they will start and where their crumpled heap of rubbish will form. Discuss with the children how they might compose the dance: by all moving together at the same time or by one person moving followed by the next and so on. Then read them the extract from 'The litter bug'. Give the children plenty of time to compose their dances and encourage good beginnings, middles and ends.

Now help the children to create a whole class dance. Ask one person from each group to repeat their movement phrase, ending in the middle of the room, followed by the second person from each group, and then the third person, so that the whole class finish in the middle of the room pretending to be a large festering, mouldy, rotting, stinking heap of rubbish. Encourage the class to think about levels in the final large group and to work out the shape of the heap. Ask the class to go back into their threes and start from the beginning, performing their trio dances, followed by the whole class dance.

When they have performed their dance, discuss with the children what it feels like to perform a whole class dance. How is it different from performing in small groups? What additional considerations do they have to make when working together in such a large number?

Learning outcomes

In this lesson the children are involved in the interrelated processes of composing, performing and appreciating. These are the learning outcomes of this lesson and form the basis of assessment criteria linking into the Programme of Study (Common and General Requirements) and Programme of Study (Dance) in the National Curriculum.

Composing
• Explore, invent and select dance movements.
• Shape a simple dance.

• Respond to a range of stimuli: objects and literature.

Performing
• Link body actions.
• Use narrow, wide, curled, twisted body shapes.
• Make changes in level.
• Work in small groups.
• Work as a whole class.
• Perform and repeat simple dance phrases.

Appreciating
• Appreciate in simple terms the aesthetic quality of dance.

Follow-up ideas
There is sufficient material provided in this dance idea for several sessions. Follow-up this idea by discussing the fate of the rubbish heap, perhaps it will be swept up by a bulldozer and compressed into a small pack or bale. How

would this affect the children's group shape?

Continue the theme by discussing noise, water and atmospheric pollution and their effects on the environment. For example, the class could make a tape of the noise in a busy street and use this as a starting point for a dance, with all types of transport coming and going, making contrasts between movement and stillness, fast and slow, and noise and silence.

For water pollution, the class could consider the movement of flotsam and jetsam, or the changing shapes of oil on water, its dispersal after a spillage and its effects on the environment.

3. Contrasting landscapes

Age range
Nine to eleven.

Movement content
What – Body shapes.
How – Strong and light, quick and slow.
Where – Levels.
With whom – Groups.

Group size
Groups of five.

What you need
Chosen stimulus: visual, e.g., paintings, pictures or photographs of contrasting landscapes including features such as rock formations, mountain peaks or rolling downs; musical accompaniment, e.g., *Music for Dance (Tape III)* by C. Benstead (Music for Dance, PO Box 727, London, SE18 3DX) or *Tubular Bells* by M. Oldfield (Virgin) or music by J.M. Jarre.

What to do
Introduction
Ask the class to run on the spot and then run to another space and run on the spot. Tell them to keep the running steps quick and light. Tell them each to find a space, well away from anyone else, and then make any stretched shape into the space and hold this shape still. Encourage them to improve their stretch, by extending their feet, lengthening their backs and stretching their fingers, and then to relax. Now ask them to make another, different stretched shape, demonstrating the same tension as before. Tell the children to put these actions together so that they run to a space and make a stretched shape, hold it still for a few seconds and then run into another space to make the different stretched shape. When the children pause to make a shape in space, encourage them to use a variety of levels and different parts of their bodies.

Movement development
Ask the children to make individual 'spikey', 'angular', 'rugged' shapes and hold these shapes very still. Let them try to make several angular body shapes, balancing on different body parts and using a variety of levels. Now tell them to make several curved shapes, again balancing on different body parts and using a variety of levels.

The children should now

incorporate travelling with the movements. Ask them to travel anywhere in the room, touch the ground, turn and make a spikey shape. Then ask them to travel around the room, touch the ground and make a curved shape, followed by travelling, touching the ground, turning and making a body shape of their choice. Encourage them to hold their body shapes for a few seconds at the end of each phrase. Repeat the three phrases to enable them to practise making their movements flow from one to the other.

Ask the class to get into groups of five and see if each group can make a solid shape where only four feet, three hands, one back and one bottom within the group are in contact with the floor. Now suggest that they make a spikey, angular, jagged group shape by linking and joining together: for example, the elbow of one child might link into the knee of another member of the group or another child might lean back against someone else's hands. Encourage the children to use

different levels. Using the words: 'smooth', 'curved', 'ongoing' and 'undulating', ask the groups to make different rounded group shapes, creating holes and spaces, sometimes making the group shape compact and sometimes elongated. Finally, let the groups try to create shapes where all the members support each other so that if one person within the group moved away the whole group would collapse.

Dance idea
Talk to the class about the changing landscapes as they travel from one part of the country to another; from the peaks of the Lake District to the undulating Yorkshire moors and Berkshire downs, from the Welsh valleys and river plains to the rugged cliffs of the coast. Show the class a variety of paintings and photographs of contrasting

landscapes.

Ask the groups to use the four different group shapes they have been working on, and move from one group shape to the next to show contrasting and changing form. Let them decide in which order they will perform their shapes and how they will move from one shape to the next. For example, they could all move together or they could move one at a time. Encourage them to think about and develop the movements between each group shape by changing levels, adding a turn, changing their body shapes or moving on different body parts. Ask each group to think about how they will start and finish. When the groups have choreographed their dances play the chosen musical accompaniment of contrasting

sounds and forms as a background to the dances. The dance does not have to 'fit' the music. When the groups have practised their dances let them perform for the rest of the class. Ask individual children to describe the dance they have just observed, and see if they can answer some of the following questions: 'Was there a contrast between the group shapes?' and/or 'Did they show a change in level?' and/or 'Did they show a range of dynamics?'

Learning outcomes

In this lesson the children are involved in the interrelated processes of composing, performing and appreciating. These are the learning outcomes of this lesson and form the basis of assessment criteria linking into the Programme of Study (Common and General Requirements) and Programme of Study (Dance) in the National Curriculum.

Composing

• Explore, invent, select and refine dance movements.
• Shape a simple dance with a clear structure.
• Respond to a range of stimuli: pictures and music.

Performing

• Link body actions.
• Use narrow, wide, curled, twisted, extended and contracted body shapes.
• Show quality of movement with a range of dynamics.
• Work in small groups.
• Perform and repeat a simple dance.

Appreciating

• Use appropriate vocabulary to describe dance.
• Show sensitivity when appraising others.

Follow-up ideas

This dance idea can be further extended by considering: industrial landscapes, buildings and skylines; rock formations, volcanoes and glaciers; erosion of the coast by the elements and by human activity; motorways; and the disappearing rainforests.

For example, look at paintings by L.S. Lowry of industrial landscapes and bring parts of the picture to life: the factory, the machines, the workers, the noise, the heat, the energy, the dirt. Always remember not to encourage the children to act out the scenes, but pick out actions and movements for them to develop.

CHAPTER 9

Fire

'Fire' is a topic that links well with science and physical properties; with physical, human and environmental geography; with festivals and celebrations in religious education; with stories and writing newspaper-style reports in English; with various uses of media such as painting or fabric printing in art; and with composition in music. 'Fire' lends itself to movement and dance too and in the dance-specific topic web for 'Fire', on page 98, movement possibilities are shown that link dance to many areas of the curriculum. The topic web considers fire in the context of: customs, festivals and celebrations, for example the fireworks and bonfires associated with Bonfire night and the Chinese New Year; stories, especially myths and legends about dragons and other fiery fantasy creatures; the uses and effects of fire such as fuel, home-fires, candles and disasters; and the colours and feelings inspired by fire.

The three lesson examples provided are based on dragons, forest fires and the feelings of being trapped by fire. The 'Dragons' dance is based on the Chinese New Year and the Year of the Dragon. In this lesson the youngest children are involved in making a chain dance, using the patterns and pathways and undulating movements that a dragon might make. This could lead on to the children being involved in making dragon masks or models, printing on fabric to make costumes and creating their own music to accompany the dance. The lesson on 'Forest fire' involves the children in a whole class dance creating the movements of a spreading forest fire, accompanied by the sounds of the fire composed using body percussion. The action words and movements could be developed further and link into other areas: dormant and erupting volcanoes, light and shadows, conservation and preservation of the environment. The lesson 'Trapped by fire!' uses the interaction of words and feelings to stimulate and create a dance based on the idea of being trapped and trying to escape. The dance idea involves the children working individually and in groups. This idea could be further extended into English activities, encouraging creative writing based on the children's feelings and emotions as explored in the dance lesson.

ACTIVITIES

Flames
Flickering
Olympic torch
Candle
Melting
Dripping
Burning
Forest fire
House fire
Disaster
Smoke
Fire-fighting
Great Fire of
London (1666)
Fire brigade
Fire-extinguisher
Feelings
Danger
Panic
Trapped
Comfortable
Warm

Fire

Stories
Myths and legends – dragons,
phoenix
Customs and festivals
Death ceremonies –
cremations
Bonfire Night –
fireworks
Chinese New Year –
firecrackers
Effects on:
Landscape
People
Uses
Fuels – gas, coal
Cooking
Heat
Warmth
Colours
Red, Orange
Yellow, Purple
Blue

1. Dragons

Age range
Five to seven.

Movement content
What – Whole body actions.
How – Quick and slow.
Where – Directions and levels.
With whom – Whole class and
groups.

Group size
Whole class and then small
groups.

What you need
Chosen stimulus: visual, e.g.,
pictures and photographs of
Chinese festival dragons;
chosen accompaniment:
traditional Chinese music.

What to do
Introduction
Stand with the children in a
large circle, with everybody
facing inwards and holding

hands. With the Chinese music
playing in the background,
lead the children around the
room in a long chain, weaving
in and out of the space,
making curving, coiling and
spiralling patterns on the
floor. Ask the children to
return to the circle and let go
their hands and then try to
follow you again around the
room in a long chain.

Movement development
Ask the children to walk
around the room individually,
sometimes walking high,
sometimes walking low and
moving forwards, backwards
and from side to side.
Encourage the children to
move up and down as they

make winding pathways on the
floor using curved and coiling
lines. Let them try out their
ideas to the music. Stop the
music several times to
encourage the class to move
when they hear the music and
to stop and stand still when
the music stops.

Dance idea
Divide the class into small
groups and choose a leader for
each group. Ask the children
to follow their leaders around
the room moving high, low,
forwards, backwards and from
side to side, making a chain
pattern as they go. Make sure
that the children look where

they are going and do not bump into each other or another group.

Show the children pictures of Chinese festival dragons and the dragon heads and masks used in the festival celebrations and carnivals. Play the Chinese music again and let the class listen to the different sounds. Now let the children perform their dragon dances to the music. Allow them adequate time to invent and try their ideas.

Divide the class in half and ask one half of the class to sit around the edge of the room, while the other half of the class find spaces ready to perform their dragon dances. Tell the children watching to look out for the patterns the

dancers make on the floor, and see whether the dances move up and down, forwards, backwards and from side to side. Encourage the children to talk about the dances they have seen. Then tell them to change over so that all the groups have the opportunity to perform and watch.

Learning outcomes

In this lesson the children are involved in the interrelated processes of composing, performing and appreciating. These are the learning outcomes of this lesson and form the basis of assessment criteria linking into the Programme of Study (Common and General Requirements) and Programme of Study (Dance) in the National Curriculum.

Composing
• Invent a simple phrase.

Performing
• Travelling and stepping.

• Contrast between movement and stillness.
• Move forwards, backwards and sideways.
• Move high and low.
• Show an awareness of general space.
• Copy teacher's movements.
• Perform a simple phrase.

Appreciating
• Observe and describe dance.

Follow-up ideas

When introducing these ideas for the first time, if the children are not ready to work in groups, then you, the teacher, can be the leader of the dragon dance. The dance idea can be repeated to give other children the opportunity to lead the dragon dance.

The children can be encouraged to look at the shape of the dragon's head and body and either make a mask to wear when they perform their dragon dances or use different parts of their bodies to suggest different parts of the dragon. This can then lead on to considering how the size and shape of a dragon would influence the way it would move, for example, with big, slow strong steps.

This dance idea is based on the Chinese New Year and the Year of Dragon ...1976, 1988, 2000...), but the movement ideas can easily be adapted to myths and legends such as the Chinese dragon god, the Mummers plays, 'St George and the dragon', or 'Theseus and the Minotaur'. A dragon dance could be created out of the events before St George slew the dragon or a 'Follow-my-leader' idea could be developed from the story of Theseus weaving around the labyrinth while hunting the Minotaur.

Action words			
walking	following	winding	weaving
curving	circling	meandering	coiling
spiralling	rising	sinking	undulating
flying	gliding	menacing	roaring

2. Forest fire

Age range
Seven to nine.

Movement content
What – Whole body actions.
How – Quick and slow, strong and light.
Where – Levels.
With whom – Individually and whole class.

Group size
Individuals, then whole class.

What you need
Chosen stimulus: action words, e.g. words to describe a forest fire; chosen accompaniment: body percussion.

What to do
Introduction
Ask the children to sit on the floor in a large circle, in a comfortable position where they are able to move their hands and arms freely. Tell them to rub the palms of their hands together to make a sound, starting slowly and gradually increasing the speed. Now let them try clicking their fingers; first with one hand, then with the other, and then both together. Can they beat their chests slowly to create a hollow sound? Can they clap their hands on the floor in front of their bodies?

Let the class experiment using these sounds to create a piece of body percussion music. Starting one at a time moving round the circle, tell the children to rub the palms of their hands together, so that as each person joins in the sound starts to build up. When the last person in the circle has joined in, then the person who started the sound should change to clicking his fingers, or beating his chest or slapping his hands on the floor with an irregular rhythm, in various percussive combinations, then the next person should join in and the next and so on until the whole class have joined in.

Tell the children not to make too many of the clicking sounds. The third time round the circle the children should return to rubbing the palms of their hands together with the occasional finger click, and

Action words					
curling	spiralling	rising	wavering	burning	sparking
crackling	spitting	sizzling	exploding	whirling	flying
leaping	darting	roaring	spreading	sinking	smouldering

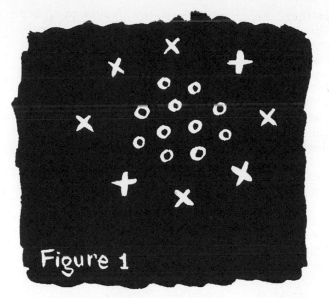

Figure 1

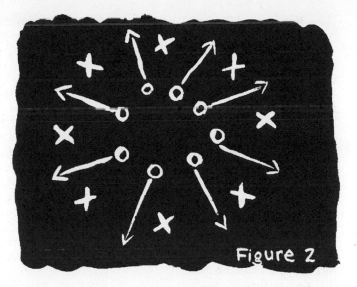

Figure 2

X = musician
O = dancer

finally, one by one, they should stop making any sound at all.

Talk to the children about forest fires and how they start and spread, and the noises that might be heard. Ask the children to think about words to describe a forest fire – the smoke, the flames and the heat. At the beginning of this lesson, there is a list of action words to help you.

Now ask the children to find spaces and start low, near the floor, in a small curled-up shape and then quickly rise up and sink down just like a flicker of light. The movement might be only of a hand or arm or a turn of a head. Repeat this idea several times, telling the children that each time they rise they should make the movement bigger. As they do this, ask the children to try leaping, jumping and darting.

Movement development

Ask the children to make short, sharp, quick, strong movements using different parts of their bodies when you click your fingers or clap your hands. Suggest that they use their feet, legs, hands, shoulders, elbows and so on. Use the words 'crackling', 'spitting', 'exploding' and 'sparking' to help the children to colour the movements. Now ask them to develop a movement phrase of rising and falling, gradually making the movements bigger and ending with leaping, jumping, darting movements and sometimes adding a quick, sharp, strong movement.

Dance idea

Divide the class into two groups. Tell half the class to sit on the floor in a large circle, leaving a space between each of them to enable a dancer to move through. Tell the other half of the class to sit in the middle of the circle (see Figure 1 above). Those in the outer circle should make

the sounds like the forest fire using body percussion, as before, while the inner group create the movements of the flickering flames. Use words such as: 'rising', 'leaping', 'darting', 'spitting', 'sparking', 'crackling', 'spreading', 'spiralling', 'sinking' and 'smouldering' to encourage the movement. As the children leap and dart encourage them to move through the spaces between the musicians and spread into the outer space before 'sinking' and 'smouldering', as in Figure 2. Let the outer group practise their sounds first while the dancers listen. If necessary, remind them of the sound ideas by revising the introduction to the lesson. The dancers need to listen very carefully to see how their movements will fit with the body percussive sounds the outer group make.

Ask the dancers to take up their starting positions, curled-up motionless on the floor. When the sounds begin the dancers should join in when they are ready. Remember the percussive sounds are an accompaniment and a stimulus for the movement and the dancers may have to adapt their movement phrases and respond to the sound. At first both the groups will need some guidance; when to start, when to change a sound, when to leap, when to stop and so on. However, it is important that the class perform their piece of work themselves. The key person in the class will be the musician who starts the whole composition. When they have finished their dance, discuss with the children whether they want to make any improvements, where there are strengths and where there are weaknesses and whether they would like to perform it again, trying to incorporate these changes.

Learning outcomes

In this lesson the children are involved in the interrelated processes of composing, performing and appreciating. These are the learning outcomes of this lesson and form the basis of assessment criteria linking into the Programme of Study (Common and General Requirements) and Programme of Study (Dance) in the National Curriculum.

Composing
• Explore, invent, select and refine dance movements.
• Shape a simple dance with a clear structure.
• Respond to a range of stimuli: body percussion and words.

Performing
• Link body actions.
• Isolate body parts.
• Show a range of dynamics.
• Make changes of level.

• Work as a whole class.
• Perform and repeat simple dance phrases.

Appreciating
• Use appropriate vocabulary to describe dance.
• Appreciate in simple terms the aesthetic quality of dance.

Follow-up ideas
This dance idea will take more than one session to complete and it is very important to change over the groups so that all pupils have the opportunity to be dancers and musicians. If the class find this idea difficult, work on exactly the same ideas, but put the children in twos so that one becomes the musician and the other becomes the dancer and vice versa. In this way, the children will have more time to experiment and select ideas and practise their movements before going on to a whole class dance. The sounds the children create could be taped and used as the accompaniment to which the whole class could dance. As a follow-up to this, the children could use percussion instruments to create alternative sounds to accompany the movement.

3. Trapped by fire!

Age range
Nine to eleven.

Movement content
What – Body shapes.
How – Quick and slow, straight and roundabout, stopping and continuous.
Where – General space, levels and directions.
With whom – Individuals and groups.

Group size
Individuals, then groups of six.

What you need
Paper, pens or pencils.

What to do
Introduction
Ask everyone in the class to find a space, and become aware of where they will move in the room, looking where they are going and avoiding collisions. Tell them to run somewhere in the room, freeze, move backwards slowly and then run somewhere else, freeze and move backwards slowly, and then run somewhere else and freeze. Repeat this idea. Tell the children to imagine that they cannot get out of the room, whatever they try to do. Ask them to think about how they would feel and move and encourage them to show the contrast between rushing and retreating slowly.

Movement development
Ask the children each to find a space and balance on one leg in a large, stretched, wide shape, then overbalance, fall, roll across the floor and get back up on to their feet, ready to start again. Talk to the

Action words		
rushing	retreating	rolling
jumping	trapping	pushing
falling	balancing	overbalancin
motionless	panicking	rescuing

children about how they might fall safely so that they do not hurt themselves. Encourage them to try falling forwards, backwards and sideways, using their arms and hands to break their fall and bending their legs to lower their body weight to the floor. Repeat this movement phrase several times and ask them to try balancing on parts of their bodies other than their feet. Now let them try to put the following movements together: rush across the room, freeze, move backwards slowly, balance, fall, roll, get back up on to their feet ready to start again.

Ask the children to get into groups of six. In each group, five of the group should hold hands in a circle with the sixth person in the middle. Now tell the person in the middle to try to get out of the enclosed circle. The group meanwhile have to try and prevent the person in the middle from escaping by changing levels. Change over who is the sixth person regularly, so that everyone in each group has the experience of being in the middle.

Dance idea
Give each group a sheet of paper and a pen or pencil and ask them to discuss and write down all the words they can think of to describe how they might feel if they were trapped in a building, or on an aeroplane, or on an oil rig or in a boat, which was on fire and were trying to escape. Let each group share their list of words with the class and explain why they have chosen them.

Now talk about the dance idea. Working individually, ask the children to use the following words and phrases and put them into a movement phrase: 'rush', 'freeze', 'move backwards', 'overbalance', 'roll', and 'move across the floor as low as possible'. At the same time, ask them to think about how they might feel if they were trapped by fire; for example, scared, frightened, helpless, terrified, panicky, courageous, or strong. Repeat the final movement phrase several times so that the children can refine their dance movements.

...e class to get into ...groups again and, in each ...p, decide who is going to ...e the person to be trapped. Tell the rest of each group to join hands and make an 'open' circle (see Figure 1 below). Then ask each of the chosen 'trapped' people to rush into the open group, freeze, move back slowly, and try to rush in somewhere else, but the group circle should now close and trap them (as in Figure 2). Then the trapped people must try to get out. Let the groups decide how their dances will finish – will the trapped people escape? How will they escape? Now tell the children to go back to the beginning and start again with the individual phrases and finish with the group ideas. It will be important to make sure that the groups end together in an open circle after they have finished their individual phrases, ready to make their catch. Encourage the children to make sure their dances have clear beginnings (where will they start?), good middles (how do they move?) and interesting ends (where will they finish?). Let each group show their dance to the rest of the class. Ask the audience if the dance shows fear and encourage them to discuss what they saw using appropriate dance vocabulary.

Learning outcomes
In this lesson the children are involved in the interrelated processes of composing, performing and appreciating. These are the learning outcomes of this lesson and form the basis of assessment criteria linking into the Programme of Study (Common and General Requirements) and Programme of Study (Dance) in the National Curriculum.

Composing
• Explore, invent, select and refine dance movements.
• Shape a simple dance with a clear structure.
• Respond to a range of stimuli: words and feelings.
• Create dances which communicate feelings.

Performing
• Link body actions.
• Show quality of movement with a range of dynamics.
• Work in small groups.
• Perform and repeat simple dance phrases.

Appreciating
• Use appropriate vocabulary to describe dance.
• Appreciate in simple terms the aesthetic quality of dance.
• Show sensitivity when appraising others.

Follow-up ideas
Ask the children to think of other situations that happen in our everyday lives at home, or in the wider world around us, (such as arguments, accidents, disasters, celebrations, successes and failures) which involve individuals or groups conveying a variety of feelings.

Encourage the children to discuss other moods and emotions, such as anger, rage, happiness, sadness, being proud, feeling rejected and so on. Suggest that they relate their movements to the feelings; for example rage could inspire quiet, strong, explosive movements, whereas calm might be shown by slow, light, swaying, undulating and turning movements.

The idea of different colours conveying different moods and feelings could also be developed. For example, fiery red might suggest strong turning jumps and leaps, cool blue might lead to slow, controlled movements, while purple is regal, green is tranquil, yellow is warm and so on.

A further idea on this theme is developed in Chapter 17, 'People and places', in the nine- to eleven-year-olds lesson, 'Moods, feelings and emotions' on page 173.

Figure 2

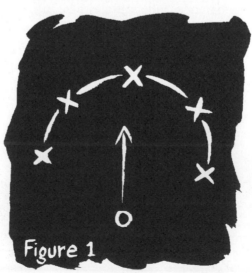

Figure 1

CHAPTER 10

Air

'Air' is one of the four classical elements, and has become an important topic in the primary school, particularly since the introduction of science as a core subject within the National Curriculum.

The dance-specific topic web for 'Air', on page 106, shows a variety of areas that lend themselves to exploration through movement: the varying force of the wind; how the temperature can affect our movements; how birds and objects move in flight; aerobic exercise; and the influence of gravity and the movements of the planets.

The three example lessons provided are all based on flight and demonstrate the use of a variety of starting points. The 'Balloons' lesson uses the idea of a balloon being blown up gradually, of it drifting and floating and, eventually, falling to the ground where it bounces before finally bursting. The 'Birds' lesson focuses on the way birds hover, glide, dive and swoop and then explores formation flying. The stimulus for this lesson is an extract from the story Jonathan Livingston Seagull by Richard Bach. The final lesson explores the idea of kite flying and the different shapes of the kites and the patterns that they make in the air. This uses both action words and actual kites of different shapes to stimulate dance ideas.

All of the lessons include the processes of composing, performing and appreciating as required by the National Curriculum programmes of study and would lend themselves to follow-up work across the curriculum. Cross-curricular links might include: the history of flight, famous pilots and aircraft; aerodynamics in science and, in technology, designing and building a model that can fly, for example a kite. Flight could also be explored in gymnastics, through making different body shapes while in the air.

ACTIVITIES

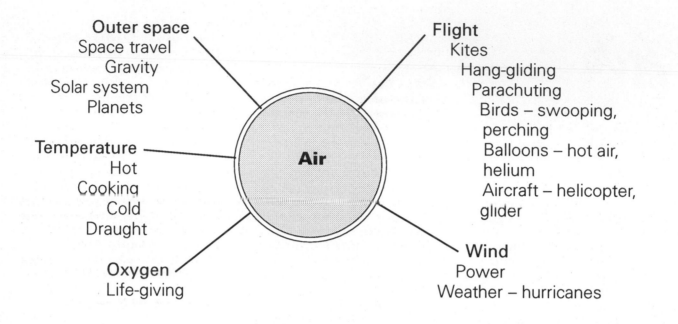

Outer space
Space travel
Gravity
Solar system
Planets

Flight
Kites
Hang-gliding
Parachuting
Birds – swooping,
perching
Balloons – hot air,
helium
Aircraft – helicopter,
glider

Temperature
Hot
Cooking
Cold
Draught

Air

Oxygen
Life-giving

Wind
Power
Weather – hurricanes

1. Balloons

Age range
Five to seven.

Movement content
What – Body shapes.
How – Light and quick or slow.
Where – General space and
levels.
With whom – Teacher and the
class.

Group size
Individuals.

What you need
Chosen stimuli: objects, e.g., a
balloon, a picture of a balloon
seller (photocopiable page
183); tambourine;
photocopiable page 184.

What to do
Introduction
Ask the children to stand in
their own spaces, with their
feet close together, and keep
very still. Then ask them to
bounce on the spot still
keeping their feet together.
Make sure that they are
bouncing so that their heels
lift off the floor first and then
their toes, so that they are
flexing their ankles. Their toes
should only just lift off the
floor and their heels should
touch the floor each time they
land. Encourage the children
to use their knees to help
them to bounce. When you see
that they are all bouncing
correctly, ask the children to
see if they can travel around
the room and still bounce with
their feet close together.
Remind them always to look

for a space and avoid bumping
into each other as they move
around. Encourage them to
bounce 'here, there and
everywhere' and to try to
bounce in different directions.
Now ask the children to
stand still and listen while you
play a simple rhythm on the
tambourine, such as: 1, 2, 3; 1,
2, 3; 1, 2, 3; stop. Repeat the
rhythm several times so that
the children become familiar
with it. When you feel that
they are confident with the
rhythm, tell them to try to
bounce in time as you play.

Movement development
Ask the children each to find a
space on their own, away from
anyone else, and to make
themselves as small as
possible; so that they are
making small, rounded body
shapes. Now ask them to make
large shapes with their bodies

and hold these shapes very still. Their large shapes may be made so that most of their bodies are in contact along the floor, or it may be that just their feet are on the floor. Let them repeat their small shapes and then change to their large shapes, so that they experience the difference between being large and being small.

Now ask the children to come and sit down on the floor near you so that they can all see you clearly. Take a balloon and blow it up with four large puffs. Encourage the children to observe and comment upon the size of the balloon as it gradually changes from small to large as the air is blown into it. Tell the children to return to their spaces and make their small body shapes. Explain that you are going to count slowly from one to four and as you count they are to gradually make their body shapes larger, as if they are being blown up like a balloon, so that on the count of four they have reached their large

shapes. Repeat this idea several times, always starting from the small shapes, so that the children can begin to estimate how much bigger they should make their body shape on each count. Let half the class watch while the others perform this movement phrase. Encourage them to observe how large they need to be on each count. Then swap over, to let the other half of the class observe. The children may like to accompany their movements by making four blowing noises as they gradually increase their body shapes in size.

Now introduce the idea of travelling around the room slowly and lightly, with the children moving around each other and sometimes changing level, so that some of the children may be stretching high while others may be bending low as they pass by each other.

Now encourage them to put these two movements together; changing from small to large shapes to four counts and then moving about the room.

Dance idea
Show the children a picture of a balloon seller holding all the strings of the balloon so that they do not float away (such as photocopiable page 183). Ask the children to start all around you in their small, rounded shapes, like the balloons all in a bunch around the balloon seller. Tell them that the strings are all different lengths, so that some of the children can be nearer to you than others. To the count of four, or to their own puffing sounds, tell them to increase the size of their body shapes

one, two, three....

Action words					
expanding	enlarging	growing	increasing	filling	contracting
shrinking	reducing	diminishing	changing	bouncing	bobbing
rising	falling	sinking	floating	drifting	weaving
meandering	bumping	bursting	popping	exploding	tugging

gradually, as if they are a giant bunch of balloons being inflated ready to be sold. A few at a time, let some 'float away', drifting freely and slowly in and out around each other. Ask the children to join in so that eventually everyone is moving slowly around everyone else and changing levels as they go. Now ask them all to begin to sink down to the floor as you start to play the rhythm on the tambourine, so that they can bounce to the rhythm (1, 2, 3; 1, 2, 3; 1, 2, 3) and then pretend to burst. Encourage them to keep in time and to make the 'burst' a sudden surprise.

When the children return to the classroom, give each child a copy of photocopiable page

184 and ask them to draw on it the size and shape of their balloon at each of the four stages and write in the space provided why their balloon might have burst. Drawing the gradual increase in size of the balloon will reinforce the way that the children had to gradually increase their body shapes in size during the dance and will remind them of what they pretended had made the balloon burst.

Learning outcomes
In this lesson the children are involved in the interrelated processes of composing, performing and appreciating. These are the learning outcomes of this lesson and form the basis of assessment criteria linking into the Programme of Study (Common and General Requirements) and Programme of Study (Dance) in the National Curriculum.

Composing
• Invent and adapt a simple phrase.
• Experience a range of stimuli (object).

Performing
• Contrast between large and small shapes.
• Move high and low.
• Travelling, jumping.
• Respond to simple rhythms.
• Use of repetition.

Appreciating
• Observe and describe using appropriate dance vocabulary.
• Show sensitivity to others when watching dance.

Follow-up ideas
The children could explore a variety of different body shapes using a bag of party balloons of different shapes and sizes as the stimulus.

Let them observe a balloon being blown up again, but instead of just letting the air out so that it can be blown up again, let go of the balloon when it is inflated and encourage the children to comment upon how it rushes quickly from side to side as the air escapes, before landing and lying still and deflated on the floor. Ask the children to try to remember their way of starting small and gradually getting larger, but this time see if they can wiggle quickly from side to side before they return to the floor and their starting shapes.

2. Birds

Age range
Seven to nine.

Movement content
What – Whole body actions.
How – Quick or slow.
Where – Personal and general space.
With whom – Individuals and small groups.

Group size
Individuals, then small groups of three.

What you need
Chosen stimuli: literary, e.g. extracts from *Jonathan Livingston Seagull: a story* by Richard Bach (on page 110), and music, e.g., 'On the wing of a condor' on *Cacharpaya (Panpipes of the Andes)* by Incantation; tape recorder; photocopiable page 185.

What to do
Introduction
Ask the children each to find a space on their own and stand still. Make sure that they are well spaced around the room and then ask them to move about, travelling on their feet, and as they travel to weave in and out of each other. Make sure that they are always moving into a space and not bumping into each other. Remind them that they need to look for the spaces to move into and to be aware of all the other children when they are moving. Let them practise

moving in and out of each other and then stopping several times, to develop their awareness.

Now ask the children to think of words that can be used to describe different ways of stopping; for example, 'freeze', 'balance', 'hover' and so on. Encourage them to explore these different ways, for example balancing on their toes, or on two feet or on one foot and so on. Now let them repeat their ways of moving in and out of each other several times, but trying to stop in these different ways.

Movement development
Tell the children to return to the spaces in the room where they first started. Ask them each to focus on another spot in the room, just a short distance away. Can they move directly to these new spots and then stop? Now ask them

to return to their starting spaces as quickly as possible – can they 'dart' to them? Ask the children to repeat this idea of moving from their first spot to their second, but to think about changing their level too, starting from high to ending low. Words such as 'diving' or 'swooping' can be introduced. These can be contrasted with 'gliding' from one spot to another, with arms stretched out wide and tilting or dipping down on one side to take the body into a turn.

Dance idea
Play the music, for example 'On the wing of a condor' on *Cacharpaya (Panpipes of the Andes)* by Incantation, and ask the children to carefully listen to it. Tell them to develop a

Action words

hovering	swooping	rising	banking	fluttering	wheeling
descending	falling	swerving	spreading	looking	diving
accelerating	circling	balancing	searching	darting	speeding
turning	seeking	gliding	attracting	curving	stalling

... Flying out to his lonely practice area, folding his wings for a dive from eight thousand feet, he set himself at once to discover how to turn.

A single wingtip feather, he found, moved a fraction of an inch, gives a smooth sweeping curve at tremendous speed. Before he learned this, however, he found that moving more than one feather at that speed will spin you like a rifle ball... and Jonathan had flown the first aerobatics of any seagull on earth.

He spared no time that day for talk with other gulls, but flew on past sunset. He discovered the loop, the slow roll, the point roll, the inverted spin, the gull bunt, the pinwheel.

... They came in the evening, then, and found Jonathan gliding peaceful and alone through his beloved sky. The two gulls that appeared at his wings were pure as starlight, and the glow from them was gentle and friendly in the high night air. But most lovely of all was the skill with which they flew, their wingtips moving a precise and constant inch from his own.

Without a word, Jonathan put them to his test, a test that no gull had ever passed. He twisted his wings, slowed to a single mile per hour above stall. The two radiant birds slowed with him, smoothly, locked in position. They knew about slow flying.

He folded his wings, rolled, and dropped in a dive to a hundred and ninety miles per hour. They dropped with him, streaking down in flawless formation.

At last he turned that speed straight up into a long vertical slow-roll. They rolled with him, smiling.

short phrase to the first verse of the song using the ideas of gliding, weaving, turning and hovering. Play the music several times and let the children try their movements, giving them the opportunity to practice their ideas. Now ask them to develop a different phrase for the second verse, this time using their ideas for diving and swooping, including the change of speed and level and the different ways of balancing which they have found. Again play the music several times to allow them to repeat and clarify their ideas.

Now ask the children to sit down and then read them the extracts (see opposite page) from *Jonathan Livingston Seagull.*

Tell them to move so that they are sitting in groups of three. Give each group a copy of photocopiable page 185 to look at the trio formations given there and then let them try out these formations in their dances. Using some of the ideas mentioned in the extract from *Jonathan Livingston Seagull,* can they develop their version of precision flying? They should include at least two different formations in their dances.

Allow the children enough time to develop their dances. When they are quite clear about how their dances start and finish and their chosen formations, encourage them to show and share their dance ideas with the rest of the class. When each group has finished performing, ask those watching to show you, by pointing to the photocopiable page, the formations that the group used and describe how they used each of the formations. On returning to the classroom, the children can circle the formations that they included and draw any others that they can think of that could have been included on the photocopiable page. This page can be used as evidence for assessment, to show that the children understand that trios can use a variety of different formations and what these might be.

Learning outcomes
In this lesson the children are involved in the interrelated processes of composing, performing and appreciating.

These are the learning outcomes of this lesson and form the basis of assessment criteria linking into the Programme of Study (Common and General Requirements) and Programme of Study (Dance) in the National Curriculum.

Composing
• Create dances which communicate ideas.
• Explore, invent, select and refine dance movements.
• Shape a simple dance with a clear structure.
• Respond to a range of stimuli: words and music.

Performing
• Make changes of level.
• Link body actions.
• Work in small groups.
• Perform and repeat simple dance phrases.
• Perform dances which communicate ideas.

Appreciating
• Use appropriate vocabulary to describe dance.

Follow-up ideas
Other situations where birds might fly in formation could be discussed and explored through movement; for example the patterns for migration. Factors which may influence their flight could also be included. For example, flying against a strong head wind would result in resistance and affect their speed. You might also like to consider the effect of sighting food; the converging breakfast flock all diving in succession or the hawk or falcon spotting its prey, for example, and grabbing, clutching or snatching at it.

3. Kites

Age range
Nine to eleven.

Movement content
What – Whole body actions and body shapes.
How – Quick or slow.
Where – Levels and patterns in the air.
With whom – Individuals and with partners.

Group size
Individuals, and partners.

What you need
Chosen stimuli: objects, e.g., kites of different shapes and sizes, and action words, e.g., words to describe kites in flight; paper and pens.

What to do
Introduction
With the children standing in their own spaces, tell them to turn as fast as they can. Can they turn to the right and then turn to the left? Now ask them to turn so that they are starting high and ending low or starting low and turning to finish high.

Movement development
Ask the children to think about the different shapes that they can make with their bodies, for example stretched wide, long and thin or symmetrical, and to show you some of these shapes. Ask them each to select one shape and then to travel a few steps and jump into the air, showing the shape that they have selected. Tell them to repeat this idea of running and jumping as they show different shapes in the air. Make sure that they always land safely. Now ask them to select a turning jump and to repeat it several times, encouraging them to relate the words to their previous movement experiences. Tell them that they may use the words in any order they like to make up phrases of four movements. Ask them to think about how their phrases will start and how they will finish. Allow the children time to repeat and clarify their phrases.

Dance idea
Discuss with the class words to describe flying a kite. Write down all the words so that the class can see them clearly; perhaps on a flip-chart or wall poster.

Ask each child to find a partner and in their pairs decide who is going to be 'A' and who is 'B'. A will be flying

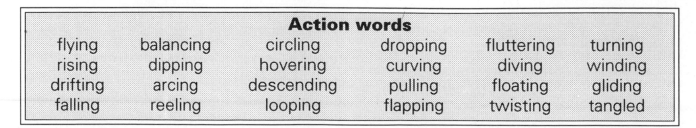

Action words					
flying	balancing	circling	dropping	fluttering	turning
rising	dipping	hovering	curving	diving	winding
drifting	arcing	descending	pulling	floating	gliding
falling	reeling	looping	flapping	twisting	tangled

the kite while B will move like the kite. Ask them to select three or four words from the class list to help them to devise a dance phrase using the idea of flying a kite. Try to encourage them to select words that show a change in speed. Tell them that they may repeat some of the words to make up a rhythmical phrase; for example, 'soar, toss, toss, glide, fall, glide, fall'. The children will also need time to discuss the shape of their kite. Show them the different shapes and sizes of kites that you have collected for the

lesson and discuss the patterns that the kites could make when flying in the air. Encourage the children to try out some of their ideas in movement; they may need to change and adapt their ideas several times. In order to help them clarify their ideas, encourage them to consider the following questions:
• How does a kite get into the air?
• Is the person flying the kite always in control of it?
• How long is the string on their kites and, therefore, how near or far away they should be from their partners?
• What effect does the tension of the string have?
• What happens if the string becomes too taut or too loose?

By asking these questions, the children will be able to think clearly about what is happening in their dances as well as planning how they will start and finish.

When the children have created their dances and have had sufficient time to refine their movements, ask half of the class to show their dances while the others observe. Encourage the children to comment on the ideas they have seen before they change over.

When the children return to the classroom, give them paper and pens and ask them, with their partners, to write down and illustrate the three or four words that they selected from the class list and then how they arranged the words to form the rhythmical patterns for their dances.

Learning outcomes

In this lesson the children are involved in the interrelated processes of composing, performing and appreciating. These are the learning outcomes of this lesson and form the basis of assessment criteria linking into the Programme of Study (Common and General Requirements) and Programme of Study (Dance) in the National Curriculum.

Composing

• Explore, invent, select and refine dance movements.
• Create dances which communicate ideas.
• Respond to a range of stimuli: words.
• Shape a simple dance with a clear structure.

Performing

• Make patterns, in the air.
• Use narrow, wide, twisted and extended body shapes.
• Work with a partner.
• Perform and repeat simple dance phrases.
• Perform dances which communicate ideas.

Appreciating

• Use appropriate vocabulary to describe dance.
• Appreciate in simple terms the aesthetic quality of dance.
• Show sensitivity when appraising others.

Follow-up ideas

The children could be asked to think about how a kite, and hence their dance movements, may be affected if it was a very windy day. They could be encouraged to follow their original dance phrases with a second phrase showing how their movements and their patterns in the air would be changed by the rising wind. If the children try making and flying their own kites, they could be encouraged to draw the actual patterns made and describe how the kite moved when it was being flown in the air to use to develop their movement phrases accordingly.

CHAPTER 11

Water

'Water' is one of the four classical elements and has always been a popular and important topic area in the primary school. Capacity and volume, for example, are initially explored through infant water-play. There are also strong links with science: the water cycle, floating and sinking, uses and properties of water and water pollution, for example. The introduction of science as a core subject in the National Curriculum, the inclusion of 'Water' in other areas of the curriculum, such as physical and enviromental geography, and the importance of swimming, as part of physical education, indicate that 'Water' is likley to remain an important topic.

The dance-specific topic web on page 116 shows possible areas that relate easily to movement: the changing moods of the sea; the contrasts in speed of a river; objects that float and sink; the weather; and even doing the washing.

The three lesson examples provided explore the weather (rain and storms) and life under water.

For the five to seven age range, 'Rain' has been selected and uses the idea of the rain pattering on the ground to develop rhythmic patterns, together with ideas of sheltering under an umbrella. Cross-curricular links can be made to both geography and science, through learning about the water cycle, and to maths through capacity and its measurement. Charts and graphs can be made about the amount of rain collected, identifying and recording the number of rainy days. Links could also be made to English, by encouraging the children to write poems about rain, and as part of religious education the children could be told the story of 'Noah' (Genesis 6:5–9:17).

'Under the sea', the lesson for seven- to nine-year-olds, uses coral formations as a stimulus for group structures which others can travel over, under, around and through. Here again there could be links with science, investigating water plants and animals, and also with art, through looking at the natural formations of shells and rocks and creating coral-like structures using wire and papier mâché. Links might also be made to English, and possibly history,through stories of under sea adventures and shipwrecks, such as the Mary Rose. Contrasting life on board ship in appropriate historical and modern times could also be brought into this topic.

'The Storm' lesson for nine- to eleven-year-olds uses action words describing a storm at sea to stimulate the children's movement. Again cross-curricular links could be made to both science and geography, through studying coastal erosion, tides and flooding. Newspaper articles concerning storm damage could be collected as well as reading, telling and writing stories about storms.

ACTIVITIES

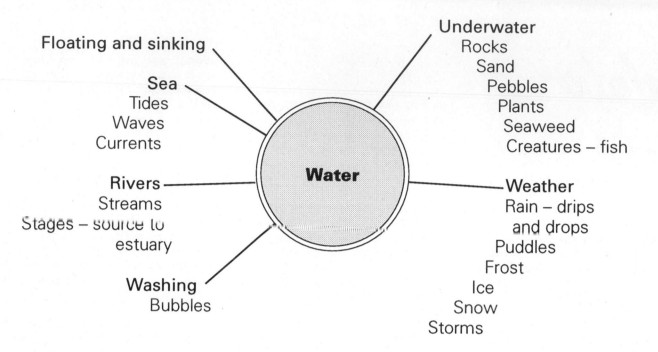

Floating and sinking

Sea
Tides
Waves
Currents

Underwater
Rocks
Sand
Pebbles
Plants
Seaweed
Creatures – fish

Rivers
Streams
Stages – source to
estuary

Water

Weather
Rain – drips
and drops
Puddles
Frost
Ice
Snow
Storms

Washing
Bubbles

1. Rain

Age range
Five to seven.

Movement content
What – Body parts, moving and stopping.
How – Quick and light.
Where – General space and levels.
With whom – Individuals.

Group size
Individuals.

What you need
Chosen stimulus: rhymes, e.g., 'Doctor Foster', or 'I hear thunder'; photocopiable page 186.

What to do
Introduction
Ask the children to make sure that they are not standing too near to anyone else and then walk slowly around the room, weaving around each other as they go, but without touching anyone. Encourage them to move slowly and to look carefully for spaces into which to move. Now ask them to repeat this, but this time a little faster, so that they are dodging in and out of the spaces. Remind them to keep alert and be ready to dodge so that they avoid bumping into anyone.

Divide the class in half. Ask one half of the class to stand still while the others dodge in and out around them. Encourage the children who are standing still to watch how well those who are moving are dodging in and out. Let them change over so that everyone has a turn at standing and watching and at dodging. Can the children comment upon their observations?

Movement development
Ask the children to find spaces and stamp their feet on the spot. Tell them to start slowly and gradually get faster. Now ask them to repeat this idea, but trying to be aware of the pattering sound of their feet on the floor. Next ask the children to stretch up really high, rising up on their toes, and to contrast this with crouching really low, so that they are close to the floor. When they are crouching low, tell them to use their hands to make the pattering sound on the floor. Ask them to explore other parts of their bodies

against which they can make the pattering sound with their hands. Tell them to select four different body parts to touch in turn, using just one beat for each part; for example, hands, knees, legs and back. Repeating this movement phrase three times will lead to a simple rhythm.

Dance idea

Read the chosen poem and tell the children to listen carefully to it. Do they think they could perform the rhythm to the poem on different body parts? Say the poem whilst the children try their rhythms on different body parts and repeat several times.

Now divide the class in half and identify which half of the class will move first and which will move second. The first half of the class should stretch high on their toes with their hands reaching up and then drop and beat their hands on the floor. Meanwhile the second half of the class should stand still. The first half of the class should stay crouching low now, while the second half of the class stretch high on their toes and then drop and beat their hands on the floor. When the second half of the class have finished beating their hands on the floor, all of the class should travel around the room quickly and lightly, dodging in and out of each other. Finally tell the children to stop and make an individual shape; it may be crouching under an umbrella, holding an umbrella or actually trying to make an umbrella shape with their bodies. Let them try out various ideas for their final shapes and then select one each, making their chosen shapes very clear. To finish the first part of the dance, ask the children to all stretch up high together and then drop and all beat their hands on the floor.

When the children return to the classroom, ask them to try to remember the four different body parts that they used for their rhythmic phrases in their dances. Give them copies of photocopiable page 186 on which to record the four parts that they used by drawing circles around them on the page. Underneath this, ask each of them to try and draw a picture of themselves in their final shape: under the

Action words					
dripping	flowing	meandering	falling	dropping	rippling
rushing	disappearing	splashing	swirling	gushing	drying
sploshing	whirling	gurgling	paddling	spraying	turning
surging	wading	soaking	spitting	drizzling	sheeting

umbrella, holding the umbrella or making an umbrella shape.

Learning outcomes

In this lesson the children are involved in the interrelated processes of composing, performing and appreciating. These are the learning outcomes of this lesson and form the basis of assessment criteria linking into the Programme of Study (Common and General Requirements) and Programme of Study (Dance) in the National Curriculum.

Composing

• Invent, select and adapt a simple phrase.
• Experience a range of stimuli (rhymes).

Performing

• Contrast between movement and stillness.
• Demonstrate the difference between fast and slow movements.
• Work without interfering with others.
• Respond to simple rhythms.
• Use of repetition.

Appreciating

• Observe and describe using appropriate dance vocabulary.
• Show simple ways of recording dance.

Follow-up ideas

Introduces the idea of splashing in puddles. The children should be encouraged to jump into a space where they have decided that their puddle may be or to kick as if they were splashing someone nearby. Alternatively, they could jump over the imagined puddles. These movement ideas could be used with a tape-recorded sound effect of the rain falling. Alternatively, percussion can be used either by you, the teacher, to accompany the dance or pre-recorded by the class after they have explored appropriate percussive sounds. Other well-known rhythms and rhymes could also be used, such as: 'Rain, rain, go away! Come again another day.' Strong rhythmic stamping steps could be used to accompany this rhyme and contrasted with light steps or fingertip taps on the floor or body for the pitter-patter sound of the drops starting to fall.

Action words					
darting	undulating	sinking	hovering	diving	opening
floating	flicking	meandering	closing	plunging	skimming
drifting	rising	swimming	waving	falling	gliding

2. Under the sea

Age range
Seven to nine.

Movement content
What – Body parts, moving successively.
How – Quick and slow.
Where – General space and levels.
With whom – Partners and small groups.

Group size
Partners and then groups of four.

What you need
Chosen stimulus: objects or visual, e.g., examples or pictures of coral, and music, e.g., 'Sleepy shores' (Theme for *Owen MD*) by J. Pearson on *Your Top TV Themes* (EMI) or 'The Aquarium' from *Carnival of the Animals* by C. Saint-Saëns; tape recorder.

What to do
Introduction
Ask the children to travel around the room, weaving in and out of each other as they go. Next tell each child to find a partner and then, in their pairs, to decide who is going to be the leader first. Can they now travel around the room, one behind the other, weaving in and out of everyone as they go? Encourage them to sometimes include a change of level. The person who is following should try to follow exactly the same pathway as the person leading the movement. Remind the children to change over so that they have experience of both leading and following movements.

Movement development
Still with their partners, ask the children to find another pair, so that they are now working in a group of four and to number themselves one, two, three and four. Number one is going to move first and should think about how he will move his arms. His movement will then be copied by number two, followed by number three and finally by number four, to give successive movement. Ask the children to repeat this idea using a different body part and then changing levels. Encourage them to have a new leader each time. Now ask the current leader to make a large, stretched-out shape. The next child should then also make a

stretched-out shape and join on to the leader. The other two children should follow on by each making a shape and joining on too, so that all four children are now joined together, each making their own large, stretched shape.

Ask the children to see if they can create different shapes now and include changes of level, so that not all of them are at the same height in each group. Encourage them to look at the group structure that they have made and notice the spaces created within the structure.

Dance idea

Now ask each group of four to find another, so that there are groups of eight, each with a group A and a group B. Show the children some examples or pictures of coral so that they can see the shapes created. Ask the group As to create group structures, thinking particularly of different levels and spaces in order to develop a branch-like structure using the image of coral. At the same time that the A groups are creating their coral structures, the B groups should spread out individually and start weaving and darting around the room. As they travel, encourage them to gradually find the other members of their group and to follow one behind the other, so that eventually all of each group B are in a line, following one behind the other, darting and weaving around the room like a shoal of fish. When each group A have formed their coral structure, their group B can begin to look for spaces in it where they can travel over, under, around and through the coral shape.

Ask the children to show and share their ideas and encourage them to comment upon the different coral-like structures that have been created and how the B groups used the spaces. Their attention can be drawn towards the different levels used in the structures and the way the individuals chose to join on to the groups or the pathways that the groups created as they travelled over, under, through and around the spaces created.

Learning outcomes

In this lesson the children are involved in the interrelated processes of composing, performing and appreciating. These are the learning outcomes of this lesson and form the basis of assessment criteria linking into the Programme of Study (Common and General Requirements) and Programme of Study (Dance) in the National Curriculum.

Composing
• Explore, invent, select and refine dance movements.
• Shape a simple dance with a clear structure.
• Respond to a range of stimuli: music and visual.

• Create dances which communicate ideas.

Performing
• Isolate body parts.
• Use wide and extended body shapes.
• Work with a partner.
• Work in small groups.
• Perform and repeat simple dance phrases.
• Perform dances which communicate ideas.

Appreciating
• Use appropriate vocabulary to describe dance.
• Appreciate in simple terms the aesthetic quality of dance.
• Show sensitivity when appraising others.

Follow-up ideas
The A and B groups should be encouraged to change over so that all children are able to experience creating the coral-like structures and experience following as they travel through and around the structures.

Action words

flowing	dragging	tossing	ebbing	rippling	rushing
rising	splashing	swirling	gushing	falling	crashing
whirling	roaring	floating	lashing	turning	surging
sinking	pounding	foaming	breaking	plunging	eroding

3. The storm

Age range
Nine to eleven.

Movement content
What – Whole body actions.
How – Strong.
Where – Levels and directions.
With whom – Groups.

Group size
Groups of five.

What you need
Chosen stimulus: action words, e.g., words to describe a storm at sea; several large sheets of paper and some felt-tipped pens.

What to do
Introduction
Ask the children to find spaces and stand still and then start to travel forwards and then backwards taking a few steps each time. Tell them to repeat this several times and then ask them to try rising as they travel forwards and sinking as they travel backwards.

Movement development
Ask the children to explore and try out the movement possibilities of the words: 'swirling', 'tossing' and 'plunging'. Encourage them to try out several ideas that each word might suggest and then create a short rhythmical phrase by repeating these words several times, for example: 'Toss, toss, plunge, swirl, swirl, swirl'. Encourage them to repeat their phrases several times to build up a rhythm.

Dance idea
Tell the children to get into groups of five and then give each group a piece of paper and a felt-tipped pen and ask them to write down a list of words to describe a storm at sea. From their lists tell them to select five words for the group to compose a phrase that begins calm and gradually builds up into a storm. Encourage them to explore several ideas before deciding which movements they will use. Ask them to repeat their phrases several times in order to clarify their movements. Suggest that they use their own vocal sounds to accompany their movements where they feel it is appropriate. Each group should decide on a definite starting position which has to be held quite still until it is time for their group to start.

Decide the order which the groups will follow. Ask the first group to start their dance, while all the other groups are still in their starting positions. After a short while, ask the next group to start, followed by another and another, until all the groups are moving together, building up into a storm at sea. One by one the groups will stop, and should end back in their starting positions which they should hold quite still until all the groups have finished dancing.

Ask half the class to work and tell the other half to watch. The children observing the dance should be encouraged to look for specific criteria; for example, can they see the build up of the storm? Did the groups all have clear starting and finishing positions? Did each group work together, in unison, or did the children move one after the other, in canon, to achieve the storm effect?

Learning outcomes

In this lesson the children are involved in the interrelated processes of composing, performing and appreciating. These are the learning outcomes of this lesson and form the basis of assessment criteria linking into the Programme of Study (Common and General Requirements)

and Programme of Study (Dance) in the National Curriculum.

Composing
• Explore, invent, select and refine dance movements.
• Shape a simple dance with a clear structure.
• Respond to a range of stimuli: words.

Performing
• Link body actions.
• Show quality of movement with a range of dynamics.
• Work in small groups.
• Perform and repeat simple dance phrases.
• Perform dances which communicate moods and ideas.

Appreciating
• Use appropriate vocabulary to describe dance.
• Show sensitivity when appraising others.

Follow-up ideas

The children could be encouraged to make a list of words to describe a calm sea and then repeat the above ideas. In this way, a real contrast could be brought out in the movements to show the change from the calm to the rough sea. The children might also explore the differences in the moods and feelings developed by seeing a rough sea and a calm sea. What about the contrast in the movements and feelings of a group of people on board a ship on a calm and then a rough sea? How might they change?

To accompany this work sea shanties can be sung and/or sound effects for a calm and rough sea could be devised.

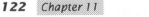

CHAPTER 12

Patterns

'Patterns' is a topic that is used regularly in the classroom and links into many area of the curriculum; for example, maths and the use of line, shape and repeating patterns; science and patterns seen in natural objects such as the spiral in a mollusc shell or the sharp lines found in a crystal; music and the use of visual patterns in musical notation; English and reading and writing, the patterns of letters and words; art and the use of shape and form, and print-making; and geography and map-making, simple orienteering in outdoor and adventurous activities and so on. In the dance-specific topic web for 'Patterns' on page 124, we show a number of possible ideas that work well in dance; for example, the patterns seen in natural objects and the elements; manufactured patterns and computer-generated patterns and grids; pathways on the floor and patterns made in the air, including lines, curves, circles and spirals; and, from design, shape and form, symmetry and asymmetry, and repeating patterns.

The three lesson examples provided are based on a journey to school, following pathways and making floor patterns. The 'Journey to school' dance idea involves the children in moving and stopping and uses moving forwards and backwards along straight and curved lines to create the pattern that the children make as they journey from home to school. This idea links well with geography through looking at routes and map-making and travelling from one place to another. The 'Pathways' lesson uses rhythm and step-patterns to create pathways on the floor and gives the children the opportunity to work together in pairs. The use of percussion encourages them to listen to and respond to the rhythmic patterns. In 'Floor patterns', the dance idea involves the children in working together in small groups to create a dance using the poem 'Lines' by Deborah Bestwick as the stimulus. Moving along straight lines and sharp angles, in different directions, should develop into an interesting floor pattern. The ideas in this lesson then link specifically to maths and geography work.

ACTIVITIES

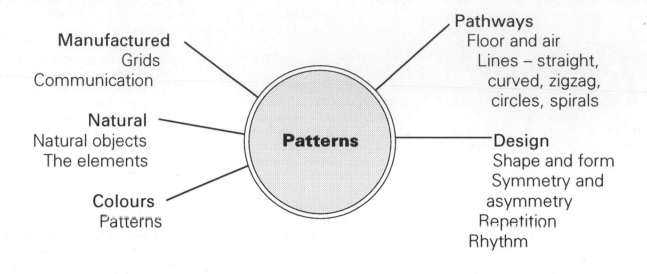

Manufactured
Grids
Communication

Natural
Natural objects
The elements

Colours
Patterns

Patterns

Pathways
Floor and air
Lines – straight,
curved, zigzag,
circles, spirals

Design
Shape and form
Symmetry and
asymmetry
Repetition
Rhythm

1. Journey to school

Age range
Five to seven.

Movement content
What – Whole body actions,
stepping.
How – Quick and slow.
Where – General space and
directions.
With whom – Individuals.

Group size
Individuals.

What you need
Paper, pens or pencils.

What to do
Introduction
Ask the children to stand
around you. Now see if they
can walk anywhere in the
space and when you say,
'Stop', stop walking and stand
still. Repeat this several times
to encourage them to move
and stop when you ask them.
Now tell them to walk close to
someone else, to walk around
the other person and then
walk away from them. Give the
children the opportunity to
practise this to increase their
awareness of moving in a large
space and moving among or
near other children.

Movement development
Ask the children to walk along
a straight line from their
starting spaces and stop. Now
tell them to walk along another
straight line and stop. Ask
them if they can move
forwards and sometimes
backwards along their lines.
Now tell them to walk along a
curved line and at the same
time try changing the speed of
their walk, sometimes moving
slowly and sometimes moving
quickly. Next tell them to walk
around a circle, moving
forwards and backwards as
they go. Finally, ask the
children if they can put all
these ideas together and walk
along a straight line
occasionally changing
direction, follow a curved line
changing speed and move in a
circle changing speed and
direction.

Dance idea
Ask the children to think about
the journey they make to
school every day. Do they walk
to school or do they travel to
school in a car, on a bus or on
a train? If they travel by car,
do they reverse out of the
drive, travel along the road,
stop at the traffic lights, turn
left or right, travel round a

roundabout? Following this discussion, encourage the children to make up a floor pattern using two or three of these ideas. Ask them to think about where in the room they are going to start their journey and where they are going to finish. Remind them to change speed and direction as they move. Let the class experiment with their ideas and then ask them to repeat their floor patterns several times, to help them to remember their journeys. When the children return to the classroom give them each a piece of paper and ask them to draw the floor patterns they made of their journeys. This can be used as a record of evidence to identify the childrens' understanding of the floor patterns they created in the lesson. The can also be used to display the variety of patterns that can be made.

Learning outcomes

In this lesson the children are involved in the interrelated processes of composing, performing and appreciating. These are the learning outcomes of this lesson and form the basis of assessment criteria linking into the Programme of Study (Common and General Requirements) and Programme of Study (Dance) in the National Curriculum.

Composing
• Invent a simple phrase.
• Show a clear beginning, middle and an end.

Performing
• Travelling.
• Contrast between movement and stillness.
• Demonstrate the difference between fast and slow movements.
• Show an awareness of personal and general space.
• Work without interfering with others.

Appreciating
• Show simple ways of recording dance.

Follow-up ideas

This dance idea could be developed by the children looking at different journeys and ways of travelling and the patterns and pathways made, for example across the sea, over the land, through the air, or up in a balloon. The children could look at: the flight of a bird and the patterns that it makes as it swoops, glides, hovers and soars through the air; the flight of a kite; the flight of a butterfly; or the flight of an aeroplane as it loops the loop. (See also the lessons on 'Birds' and 'Kites' in Chapter 10, 'Air', page 105, for flight-related dance ideas.)

Action words					
walking	jogging	running	straight	curving	zigzag
angular	twisting	slowly	fast	travelling	riding
waiting	crossing	reversing	accelerating	stopping	turning

2. Pathways

Age range
Seven to nine.

Movement content
What – Whole body actions, stepping.
How – Quick, slow, straight and roundabout.
Where – Directions.
With whom – Partners.

Group size
Partners.

What you need
Percussion instrument, e.g., claves; photocopiable page 187.

What to do
Introduction
Ask the children to begin by walking around the room, weaving around each other, so that sometimes they are far apart and sometimes close together. Now see if they can walk around the room changing their direction and speed as they go; moving forwards, backwards and sideways, sometimes walking fast and sometimes walking slow.

Movement development
Play a rhythm to the children using the percussion instrument, for example claves: quick, quick, slow; quick, quick, slow; quick, quick, quick, quick, quick, slow. Ask the children to listen to the rhythm and then to clap the same rhythm using their hands. Now ask them to stamp the rhythm on the spot using their feet. Using the same rhythm, ask them first to use their feet to travel forwards and then make their steps travel in different directions. Ask the children to think about the patterns they are making on the floor with their feet.

Dance idea
Ask each child to work with a partner and decide who is 'A' and who is 'B'. A teaches B her step pattern, then B teaches A his step pattern. When the partners are confident that they know and can perform each others step patterns, ask them to start with A's step pattern followed by B's step pattern, followed by A's and then B's. Ask the children to repeat their movement phrases several times to enable them to perform the phrase without stopping. Now tell the children to keep the same step pattern, but to try working in different ways with their partners to add variety, for example side by side, back to back, one behind the other, meeting and parting and so on. Encourage the class to practise their dances so that they have clear beginnings, middles and good endings.

Divide the class in half. Ask one half of the class to sit down and watch the other half perform their dances. Give each pair who are observing a copy of photocopiable page 187. Encourage them to watch one couple work and ask them

Action words				
weaving	meeting	backwards	following	apart
slow	parting	sideways	leading	together
quick	forwards	fast	travelling	copying

to circle on the page the ways they see the couple work together. How did they start? Did they meet and then part? Ensure the observers are given the opportunity to perform their dances.

Learning outcomes

In this lesson the children are involved in the interrelated processes of composing, performing and appreciating. These are the learning outcomes of this lesson and form the basis of assessment criteria linking into the Programme of Study (Common and General Requirements) and Programme of Study (Dance) in the National Curriculum.

Composing
• Explore, invent, select and refine dance movements.
• Shape a simple dance.

Performing
• Isolate body parts.
• Show a range of dynamics.
• Use different directions.
• Make patterns and pathways, on the floor
• Work with a partner.
• Perform a variety of rhythms.
• Perform and repeat a simple dance phrase.

Appreciating
• Use appropriate vocabulary to describe dance.
• Show different ways of recording dance.
• Show sensitivity when appraising others.

Follow-up ideas

Follow up this lesson by using the same rhythm as in the dance idea above or creating a new rhythm and using other parts of the body to make up a rhythmical movement phrase. For example, taking the rhythm: slow, slow, quick, quick, slow; the children could lift their shoulders on slow, bend their knees on slow, slap their legs on quick, click their fingers on quick and finish with a slow turn. This movement phrase could be performed individually, in pairs and in small groups. In pairs, the children could perform the movement phrase together, one at a time, or one could move and then the other, followed by both together. When the children have created their movement phrases, ask them to think about the patterns their dances are making on the floor, or give them one or several different floor patterns and see if they can perform their dances along the chosen pattern.

Action words

straight	curving	symmetry	asymmetry	chequered	zigzagging
spiralling	growing	swirling	expanding	shrinking	random
rippling	repeating	mirroring	diagonal	angular	parallel
rolling	continuous	jagged	horizontal	vertical	tangled

3. Floor patterns

Age range
Nine to eleven.

Movement content
What – Whole body actions.
How – Straight.
Where – Pathways, directions and levels.
With whom – Groups.

Group size
Groups of four.

What you need
Chosen stimuli: music, e.g., *Variations* by Andrew Lloyd Webber (MCA records), poetry, e.g., 'Lines' by Deborah Bestwick (below); photocopiable page 188 and pens; tape recorder.

What to do
Introduction
Ask the children to begin by walking around the room forwards, backwards, sideways and diagonally and occasionally changing direction. Now ask them to follow a straight line pathway along the floor and, when they change direction, ask them to make a sharp turn before moving off in another direction. Introduce the children to a rhythmic phrase, for example: walk, walk, walk, turn and change direction, walk, walk, walk, turn and change direction. Repeat this movement idea several times and encourage the children to make clear, sharp changes in direction.

Movement development
Read the first verse of the poem 'Lines' to the class. Then ask them to develop an interesting floor pattern using the lines described in the poem as a stimulus. The children should make up a phrase to last eight counts that can be repeated four times which must include travelling forwards, backwards, sideways and diagonally. Give the class adequate time to experiment,

Lines

Straight lines, long lines,
Curved lines, short lines,
Thick lines, thin lines
Horizontal, vertical,
Parallel and spiral,
Diagonal and zigzag,
All sorts of lines.

Lines for the telephone, if they cross you're in a mess,
Good strong life-lines for people in distress.
Nylon lines for fishing, don't forget the bait,
Plumb lines to hang down to see if things are straight.
Hundreds of white lines down the middle of the road,
If you don't know about yellow lines, read the Highway Code.

Railway lines, clothes lines,
Write out hundred times lines,
Lines about us all the time,
All sorts of lines.

Deborah Bestwick

select and perfect their phrases. Now ask them to think about the patterns their phrases make on the floor. Give each child in the class a copy of photocopiable page 188 and ask them each to draw their own floor pattern. Now ask the children to work with a partner and show each other the floor patterns they have drawn. Tell them to perform their partners' floor patterns. Encourage them to watch carefully and help each other to perform their partners' floor patterns accurately.

Finally, ask the children to listen to the first four phrases from the piece of music, *Variations* by Andrew Lloyd Webber and then try to perform their floor patterns to it. To add variety to their floor patterns, ask the children to introduce changes in level too.

Dance idea
Ask the children to work in groups of four and choose an area in which to work. Tell each child to decide on their starting position within that area and then trace out their floor pattern to see if they can fit all four floor patterns together without colliding with each other. Encourage the children to adapt their floor patterns if they meet someone or suggest they might pause until there is space to move again. Ask the groups to practise their dances and ensure they have included a change in level, direction and dynamics. Ask each group to show their dance to another group to help clarify the movements before sharing their dances with the whole class. The photocopiable pages can later be displayed to remind the children of the floor patterns they created.

Learning outcomes
In this lesson the children are involved in the interrelated processes of composing, performing and appreciating. These are the learning outcomes of this lesson and form the basis of assessment criteria linking into the Programme of Study (Common and General Requirements) and Programme of Study (Dance) in the National Curriculum.

Composing
• Explore, invent, select and refine dance movements.
• Shape a simple dance with a clear structure.

Performing
• Show quality of movement with a range of dynamics.
• Use different directions including diagonals.
• Make changes of level.
• Make patterns and pathways, on the floor.
• Work in small groups.

Appreciating
- Use appropriate vocabulary to describe dance.
- Appreciate in simple terms the aesthetic quality of dance.
- Show sensitivity when appraising others.

Follow-up ideas
The lesson idea described above would take several sessions to complete before the children are ready to share their work with others.

Further lesson ideas could be developed from the patterns used in board games; for example, in draughts, moving forwards, backwards and diagonally, jumping, meeting and avoiding; in snakes and ladders, moving up the ladders and down the snakes; in chess, using the patterns in the moves of each piece on the board, such as the knight which can take two steps forward and one to the side. In two groups the class could create a dance based on, for example, the game of chess. What happens in the dance when the pieces meet? Is there a battle? How does the dance end – checkmate? As a stimulus, you could use the poem, 'A game of chess' by Edith M. Stokes from *Word Pictures as a Stimulus for Creative Dance* (1970 Macdonald and Evans) and/or the music 'The Battle' from *The Legend* by Clannad (BMG Records).

A game of chess

Lined up facing are the black and white –
To attack and defend are the rules for the fight
The king is well guarded by courtiers of fame.
And a front rank of pawns, who open the game.

Each side has two castles, behind which he can hide;
If attack gets alarming, they close him inside.
His spouse is the one who can go anywhere
For long or short distances, and to any square.

The knights on their horses advance and traverse.
They are trained in set patterns, can also reverse.
To add a pious cut – with eyes set ahead,
On cornerwise pathways, the bishops do tread.

The female of the species, far deadlier than the male
Is the dominating queen, with a sting in her tail.
As she goes here and there, a trail she leaves behind
Of total destruction, presenting challenge to the mind.

Every move of each player needs great concentration –
There is much to consider with deep contemplation,
What will be the end of this battle of wits –
A win or surrender or simply quits?

Edith M. Stokes

CHAPTER 13

Machines

In order to help children to understand the impact of machines on the world in which they live and to provide them with an understanding of how things move and work, the topic of 'Machines' is a popular choice for the primary curriculum. The topic offers opportunities for cross-curricular learning particularly in technology and science, as well as being a rich source of movement and dance ideas. The dance-specific topic web on page 132 shows possible areas that relate easily to movement: the varying speeds of transport; the strength and power of machines such as steam engines contrasted with delicate micro-electronics; the range of movement possible in the human machine; the importance in everyday life of communication; and the ongoing beat of time.

'Clocks', the lesson for the five- to seven-year-old age range, uses the basic idea of starting and stopping and develops how machines tend to move to set rhythms. Cross-curricular links could be made with science and maths and how we begin to identify time; day and night and events through the day,

the week, the months and the seasons; the division of time; and telling the time by different clocks. Ways of telling the time used in the past might also be explored and modelled, for example, candle and sand clocks. In technology, the children might look at the cogs and wheels in a clock and compare how they move with other machines with which they may be familiar. Links can also be made with the various celebrations that mark the time of year.

The lesson for seven- to nine-year olds is based on the idea of the human body as a machine to develop the children's understanding of how their own bodies move. The structure of the selected music is used to form the basic structure of this dance. This lesson could be linked with music and with science (particularly Attainment Target 2) through considering the movement, the support, the muscle attachments and protection for the major organs provided by the skeleton.

In addition, pulse and breathing rates and the importance of exercise for a healthy lifestyle could be examined and could link into physical education and personal and social education.

In the lesson for nine- to eleven-year-olds the children develop human 'machines', working in groups and accompanying themselves with their own vocal sounds.

These ideas could be developed by reading stories such as Charlie and the Chocolate Factory by Roald Dahl (1985, Puffin) and, in history, the children could study inventions and the Industrial Revolution, or other appropriate period, the development of transport or how farm machines have changed over the years. While in technology, they could design and make a model of a machine for a specific purpose out of junk, and in science, they could look at forces.

ACTIVITIES

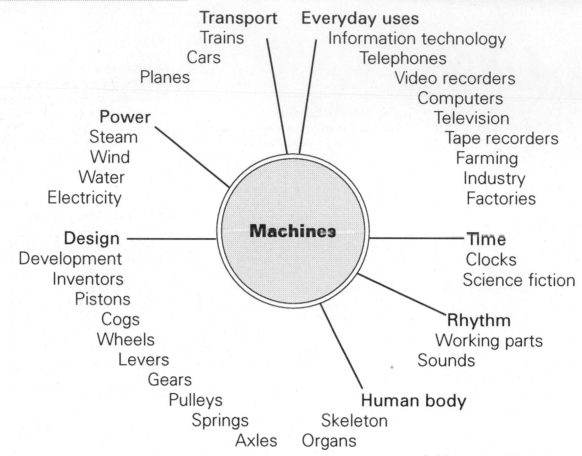

Transport
Trains
Cars
Planes

Everyday uses
Information technology
Telephones
Video recorders
Computers
Television
Tape recorders
Farming
Industry
Factories

Power
Steam
Wind
Water
Electricity

Machines

Design
Development
Inventors
Pistons
Cogs
Wheels
Levers
Gears
Pulleys
Springs
Axles

Time
Clocks
Science fiction

Rhythm
Working parts
Sounds

Human body
Skeleton
Organs

1. Clocks

Age range
Five to seven.

Movement content
What – Whole body actions.
How – Straight and roundabout.
Where – Directions and levels.
With whom – Individuals.

Group size
Individuals.

What you need
Chosen stimuli: object, e.g., a clock or watch with the insides visible, and sounds, e.g., a percussion instrument such as a wood block.

What to do
Introduction
Ask each child to stand still in a space, by themselves and away from everyone else in the room. Then ask them to walk around the room, moving around each other, and avoiding bumping into anyone by always looking for a space into which to move. Now ask the children to listen to the sound that you are going to play on the wood block and play them a 'tick-tock' type sound several times. Ask the children to still continue walking around the room, but to try to keep in time with the rhythm that you are playing. Remind them that they can walk forwards, backwards or sideways, but they must always check where they are going. Play the set rhythm (for example:1,2,3,4; 1,2,3,4; 1,2; 1,2; 1,2,3,4; stop) and ask the children to stop and change direction at the end of each phrase, as you play this rhythm several times.

Movement development
Ask the children to show you how they can turn on the spot. Can they turn on just one foot and then on two feet? Ask

Action words					
starting	winding	going	ticking	tocking	stopping
spinning	rotating	interlinking	jarring	sticking	slowing

them to think about other parts of their bodies on which they can turn. Encourage them to explore using different possible body parts and then to select one for their turning idea.

Next ask the children to stretch as high up into the air as they can, so that they are on tiptoe and their hands are reaching up to the ceiling. Now ask them to do the opposite, so that they are bending low and are really near the floor. Encourage them to repeat this idea of high and low and perhaps add a jump so that they go really high into the air. Remind them to bend their knees so that they land safely.

Dance idea

Ask the children to gather around you while you show them the inside of a clock. You may wish to do this in the classroom before the start of the lesson. If so, remind the children about how the different parts inside the clock work: how they start and stop; how some bits spin around, while other bits move up and down.

Ask the children if they can remember how they walked in different directions to the rhythm that you played. See if they can repeat this pattern of stepping and also include the way that they decided to spin and turn and then jump up and down. So, for example, they might walk forwards for four counts, turn for four counts, jump up for two counts, crouch down for two counts and then walk backwards for four counts. They might like to accompany their movements by saying 'tick-tock' to the rhythm as they move. Allow the children time to decide on the order of their movements and then to practise them. You may wish to divide the class in half, so that one half of the class performs their dance ideas while the other half of the class watches, so that they can observe the different ways of moving and how the children are trying to keep in time with the rhythm. Encourage the children to comment upon what they have seen and then ask them to change over so that everyone has a chance to perform and to observe.

The length of the dance can be increased by one half of the class standing on the spot, moving their arms like the hands on the clock-face (that is, move and stop, move and stop) for sixteen counts, while the other half of the class are performing their dance ideas and then changing over.

Learning outcomes

In this lesson the children are involved in the interrelated processes of composing, performing and appreciating. These are the learning outcomes of this lesson and form the basis of assessment criteria linking into the Programme of Study (Common and General Requirements) and Programme of Study (Dance) in the National Curriculum.

Composing
• Invent, select and adapt a simple phrase.

Performing
• Travelling, stepping, jumping and turning.
• Contrast between movement and stillness.
• Move forwards, backwards and sideways.
• Move high and low.
• Show an awareness of personal and general space.
• Respond to simple rhythms.
• Use of repetition.

Appreciating
• Observe and describe using appropriate dance vocabulary.
• Show sensitivity towards others when watching dance.

Follow up ideas

This idea could be developed by looking at how to wind up a clock to start it going. The clock stopping could be introduced plus deciding when parts in the clock are jamming or striking. Different types of clocks and how their parts move could be discussed: digital clocks and how their numbers change, the swing of the pendulum of a grandfather clock, weather clocks alternating between fine and stormy weather, and Swiss clocks with the cuckoo popping in and out and the weights moving up and down. All could then be developed in movement. This idea could be extended by looking at a variety of clockwork toys, which again have to be wound up and then move for a limited amount of time.

2. The human body as a machine

Age range
Seven to nine.

Movement content
What – Body parts.
How – Straight and roundabout.
Where – Directions.
With whom – Partners.

Group size
Partners.

What you need
Chosen stimulus: music, e.g., 'The fossils' from *The Carnival of the Animals* (C. Saint-Saëns); tape recorder; claves or similar percussion instrument.

What to do
Ask the children to spread themselves out around the room and stand still. Tell them to watch you closely and then copy what you are doing. Show them how you can lift your right shoulder and then your left shoulder, followed by both shoulders together twice. Now ask the children to join in and do these actions with you, two or three times through. How else can they move their shoulders? The shoulders can also rotate, backwards or forwards, either one at a time or both together. Tell them to rotate their shoulders either forwards or backwards, using first one shoulder and then the other and then both shoulders together. Again, allow them to repeat the movement several times. Now suggest that the children put together the two ideas of rotating and lifting their shoulders to form their own movement phrases as you accompany them on the claves with a simple rhythm: da, da, da, da, dum; da, da, da, da, dum: da, da, da, da, da, da, dum. Repeat the rhythm and movement four times in order to allow the children to become confident with the phrases.

Movement development
Now ask the children to think about how other parts of their bodies can move. For example, their heads can move from side to side, looking to the right and then the left, their backs can bend and arch, their knees can be lifted up one at a time and their arms can swing forwards and backwards or around in circles. Encourage them to explore how their different joints and limbs can move, thinking about the seven directions of forwards, backwards, upwards, downwards, to the right or left and rotating in a circle. Then, after allowing them some time to experiment, ask them to select one particular body part and move it in only two directions, for example forwards and backwards, followed by a rotation. Again, allow them enough time to repeat and clarify their movements to develop a clear phrase.

Dance idea
Ask the children to listen carefully to the chosen music; for example, 'The fossils' from *The Carnival of the Animals*. Do they recognise the rhythm as the one that you played earlier on the claves? Ask them to try out their movement phrases four times to this rhythm. Repeat this several times so that the children become familiar with the music and how their dance phrases fit to it.

Tell the children then to find partners and decide who in their pairs will show their dance idea first while the other partner observes which directions have been selected. Let each child have a chance to dance and to observe.

Working with the same partner, tell the children each to choose two phrases. As each child will only be moving to two phrases of the music, they will need to decide who will move first. After each partner has performed his or her two phrases, one of the partners should walk around the other and take hold of a part of his or her body, such as an arm or a leg, and try and see how that part moves. For example, the first child might lift the second child's elbow and then let it drop, the second child should then react to this. There will be two phrases of the music left for the children to dance to together, they may just

decide to each perform their own ideas at the same time or they may decide on a completely new way of moving. Remind them that this dance idea is based on the human body and how it can move. Allow the children plenty of time to go through their dances and play the music several times to accompany them as they move. Encourage the children to find other pairs to whom they can show their final dances.

Learning outcomes
In this lesson the children are involved in the interrelated processes of composing, performing and appreciating. These are the learning outcomes of this lesson and form the basis of assessment criteria linking into the Programme of Study (Common and General Requirements) and Programme of Study (Dance) in the National Curriculum.

Composing
• Explore, invent, select and refine dance movements.
• Shape a simple dance with a

clear structure.
• Respond to a range of stimuli: music.

Performing
• Isolate body parts.
• Use different directions.
• Work with a partner.

Appreciating
• Use appropriate vocabulary to describe dance.
• Show sensitivity when appraising others.

Follow-up ideas
This dance idea will take more than one lesson to complete and the range of movement for every body part can be explored in other lessons to make a unit of work.

This dance idea can be extended to thinking about the major organs and how they move; for example how the lungs expand as they take in air and deflate as the air is expired or how the heart acts as a pump to send the blood around the body. Place groups of dancers around the room, each exploring the movements of an organ, as if they are parts of an enormous body.

The way that the structure of the music (A × 4, B, A × 2) has been used to support the structure of the dance could be explored and other music structures could be listened to, in order to discuss how they could be translated into movement.

3. Imaginary machines

Age range
Nine to eleven.

Movement content
What – Body parts.
How – Straight and roundabout.
Where – Directions and levels.
With whom – Groups.

Group size
Groups of six.

What you need
Chosen stimulus: visual, e.g., picture of a machine; a percussion instrument such as a tambour, photocopiable page 189.

What to do
Introduction
Ask the children to listen to the rhythm that you are going to play on the tambour and then play four bars of a $^4/_4$ rhythm. Now tell them to walk around the room to the rhythm and see if they can change direction after every four steps; so that they may, for example, walk forwards for four beats, walk sideways for four beats, walk backwards for four beats and walk forwards again for the last four beats. Play the rhythm several times so that the children can repeat their step patterns. Next, ask the children to stand still on the spot and move their arms in different directions to the same rhythm. For example, they could stretch both arms up and bring them back in close to their bodies, and then stretch both arms down and bring them back in close to their bodies. Encourage the children to try out different directions – up and down,

forward and back and side to side – using their arms only at first and then enlarging their movements by involving the use of their whole bodies.

Movement development
Now ask the children to think about using other parts of their bodies; for example, their first movement, on the count of one, may be their right arms moving up at the same time as their left knees are lifted. Encourage them to explore a variety of possibilities using different body parts and directions and then to select four different ways of moving that follow on from each other, so that they have a clear pattern that fits to the set rhythm (4 bars of $^4/_4$). In order to help the children to clarify their movements, introduce the idea of pistons and discuss how they move directly in and out or up and down. Once the children have exhausted the possible variations, ask them to think about the other parts

in a machine and how they work; for example, the cogs and flywheels that rotate and turn in different ways. Ask the children to think of a way of turning. Remind them that it need not be on their feet – can they think of a different body part that they could turn on? Encourage them also to try out ideas where their whole bodies are turning, spinning and rolling, for example. When they have selected their ideas, ask the children to add their ways of turning at the end of their previously arranged phrases so that they now have the way the pistons move for the count of four, followed by the movement selected for the cog-wheel and the whole phrase is repeated four times.

moving	going	accelerating	decelerating
turning	spinning	revolving	whirling
wheeling	pulling	propelling	pushing
pulsating	vibrating	bobbing	spluttering
stopping	braking	halting	stalling

Dance idea

Gather the children round you and show them the picture of the machine that you have selected. Discuss with them what the machine parts look like (long, round, bent, twisted, flat) what the different parts do, how they move (up, down, around, vibrate) and the ways in which the different parts of the machine interlink, so that the movement of one part affects the movement of another part.

Ask the children to get into groups of six to create their own imaginary machines using their bodies. Suggest that they could start by using some of the movement ideas that they explored earlier in the lesson, but that they need to be aware of how their movements will fit together. To help them, suggest that they show each other what they were doing previously, and then think about parts (people) working in opposition, all working at the same time or one part's (person's) movement affecting the next part's (person's) movement. Some members of the groups may even do their movements lying on the floor instead of standing up, so that the children are working at different levels. Encourage them to think about the whole space and structure of their machine. Once the groups have decided on their arrangement and have some movement ideas worked out, ask them to add their own noises to accompany their movements; such as 'thump', 'whoosh', 'clang', 'sculp', 'whirr', 'blip' and 'hiss'.

Learning outcomes

In this lesson the children are involved in the interrelated processes of composing, performing and appreciating.

These are the learning outcomes of this lesson and form the basis of assessment criteria linking into the Programme of Study (Common and General Requirements) and Programme of Study (Dance) in the National Curriculum.

Composing

• Explore, invent, select and refine dance movements.
• Shape a simple dance with a clear structure.
• Respond to a range of stimuli: sounds, pictures.
• Create dances which communicate ideas.

Performing

• Link body actions.
• Isolate body parts.
• Use different directions.
• Make changes of level.
• Perform and appreciate a variety of rhythms.
• Perform and repeat simple dance phrases.
• Work in groups.

Appreciating

• Show sensitivity when appraising others.

Follow-up ideas

This idea of creating a group machine may be developed over several lessons to form a whole unit of work. In session one, the children may be involved in exploring how a group machine might move. In session two, they could develop the shape and structure of their machines. In session three, they could work on adding accompaniment to their machines, and in session four, they might explore how their machines start and stop and then be able to perform their ideas for the rest of the class. These practical sessions can be supported in the classroom by providing the children with photocopiable page 189, on which to draw a detailed diagram of their machines and describe how they started and stopped. These sheets could then form the basis of a display or be used as design sheets for art or technology activities.

An additional idea would be to develop how the machine starts. Does one part start, which affects another part and sets it working until the whole machine is in action, or is there an operator who switches the whole machine on? Similarly, what might happen to the machine, and how does it stop? Does it just stop suddenly or grind to a halt? Does it leak a sticky substance and seize up or get faster and faster, vibrate and fall apart? Does it finally explode? Eventually, the children could show each other their group machines and how they start and stop.

CHAPTER 14

Materials

'Materials and their properties' (AT3) is one of the four attainment targets in the Science National Curriculum. Therefore, 'Materials' is a topic used by most schools and covers types, properties, the structure and uses of materials. Children should be able to make comparisons between materials on the basis of simple criteria, such as strength, hardness, flexibility and solubility. In the dance-specific topic web for 'Materials' (see page 140), the numerous movement possibilities listed show how dance can be linked into science. The topic web considers the areas of: wood and ideas that can be developed using furniture,

forestry and paper; coal and mining; clay and its properties in modelling and sculpting; fabrics and their use in the production of costume; bricks and buildings; rubber and plastics; metals and magnetism.

The three lesson examples provided are based on building, wood and paper. The 'Building' dance idea for five- to seven-year-olds involves the children in actions using strength and balance and changes in speed and levels, that would take place on a building site, such as using a wheelbarrow, mixing concrete, walking along planks and scaffolding and building with bricks. As well

as linking with science, this dance idea links with music in listening and responding, and with geography and the environment. The dance idea about wood, for seven- to nine-year-olds, involves the children in all the working actions used in preparing and using wood. This dance idea shows clearly how a miming action can be developed into a dance. This lesson could link well with geography and science through looking at the preservation of forests and conservation. The 'Paper' dance idea uses a piece of paper as stimulus for movement by looking at the properties of paper.

ACTIVITIES

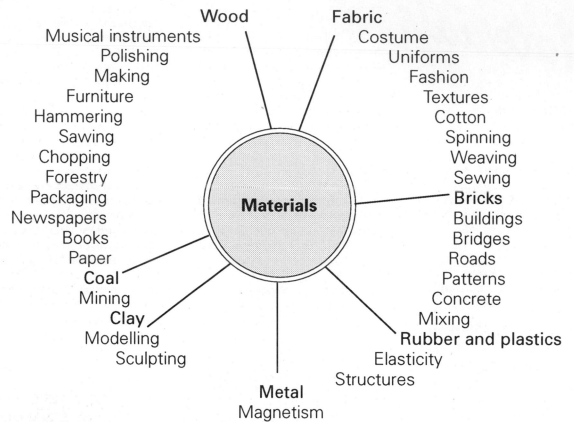

Wood
Musical instruments
Polishing
Making
Furniture
Hammering
Sawing
Chopping
Forestry
Packaging
Newspapers
Books
Paper
Coal
Mining
Clay
Modelling
Sculpting

Fabric
Costume
Uniforms
Fashion
Textures
Cotton
Spinning
Weaving
Sewing
Bricks
Buildings
Bridges
Roads
Patterns
Concrete
Mixing
Rubber and plastics
Elasticity
Structures

Materials

Metal
Magnetism

1. Building

Age range
Five to seven.

Movement content
What – Whole body actions.
How – Strong and light.
Where – Personal and general space.
With whom – Individuals.

Group size
Individuals.

What you need
Chosen stimulus: music, e.g., 'The Best of the Art of Noise' by The Art of Noise, China Records.

What to do
Introduction
Ask the children to space themselves out around the room, far away from anyone else. Tell them each to put their hands together and make a big circular movement in front of them with their arms and hands. Join in with the children so that they can copy you. Make the movement a big, strong, 'stirring and mixing' movement and repeat it four times. Now ask the children to run to another space in the room and stop. Remind them to look where they are going and avoid bumping into anyone. Can they run lightly in contrast to the strong, circular movements they made on the spot? Ask them to repeat their four big, strong, mixing movements on the spot, and then run lightly to another space and stop. Let the children perform this phrase, stirring and mixing to the first eight counts, followed by running to another space for

the next eight counts. You could perform these actions with the class to help them with the timing.

Movement development
Ask the children to see if they can walk along a straight line placing one foot in front of the other. They may need to use their arms to help them to balance. Can they walk backwards along a straight line now? This is much more difficult; ensure that they try not to bump into anyone else. See if they can walk forwards for a few steps and then turn round and walk back to where they came from, still placing one foot in front of the other, as though they were balancing on a narrow plank.

Ask the children to imagine they are lifting something very heavy and then placing it down carefully. Let them try again, this time placing the heavy object down somewhere else. With the children, experiment with the idea of lifting and placing bricks one on top of each other, starting low and getting higher each time, so that they build a tall tower. Ask the children to: 'lift and build, lift and build, lift and build, lift and build', starting low and getting higher and higher.

Dance idea
Now encourage the children to begin to put all these ideas together. They will need your help to remember what to do next. First, talk to them about the actions and movements that they might see on a building site: pushing a wheelbarrow full of sand, mixing the cement, walking along a plank and building with bricks. Tell them that to the first eight counts they can run anywhere and should then stop. To the second eight counts they should make the stirring and mixing movements. To the next eight counts they should walk and then balance followed by the building actions, starting low and getting higher and higher. Tell them to get ready to start, and ask them to, 'run and stop, mix, balance and build'. Remind them when to change from running to mixing, from mixing to balancing, and from balancing to building. Let the class try these ideas over and over again so that they become familiar with the movements. Finally, divide the class in half, and let one half of the class watch while the other half of the class perform their dance, then change over.

Action words					
mixing	churning	turning	lifting	carrying	building
balancing	smoothing	levelling	sawing	pouring	hammering

Learning outcomes

In this lesson the children are involved in the interrelated processes of composing, performing and appreciating. These are the learning outcomes of this lesson and form the basis of assessment criteria linking into the Programme of Study (Common and General Requirements) and Programme of Study (Dance) in the National Curriculum.

Composing

• Show a clear beginning, middle and an end.

Performing

• Travelling, stepping, gesture.
• Contrast between movement and stillness.
• Demonstrate the difference between strong and light movements.
• Move high and low.
• Show an awareness of personal and general space.
• Copy teacher's movement.
• Work without interfering with others.
• Perform a simple phrase.

Appreciating

• Show sensitivity towards others when watching dance.

Follow-up ideas

This dance idea might take two or three sessions to complete, especially if the sounds of a building site are created and recorded either using music or by visiting a building site. In addition, the children could look at different types of bricks and what they are made from, and the different ways of building to create a stable structure. Consider the variety, shape and size of buildings, houses, shops and tower blocks. Individually or in pairs, the children could try different body shapes and find out which shapes are stable or unstable by balancing on different parts of their bodies. Then ask the children to choose two or three different shapes and join them together.

2. Wood

Age range
Seven to nine.

Movement content
What – Whole body actions.
How – Quick and slow.
Where – Personal and general space.
With whom – Small groups.

Group size
Groups of three or four.

What you need
Chosen accompaniment: sounds, e.g., wooden percussion instruments, and/ or pre-recorded sounds of woodworking; tape recorder.

What to do
Introduction
Ask the children to move around the room using whole body actions such as travelling, turning, jumping and stopping. Encourage the children to weave in and out, avoiding each other, as they move around the room, using the whole space. Tell them to move fast sometimes and sometimes to move slowly.

Movement development
Give the children an example of a woodworking action, for example hammering a nail into a piece of wood. Ask the children to mime the action and then change the action by making it bigger. In contrast, ask them to make the action as small as they can. Now encourage them to try the action varying the size each time. Ask the children how else they might change their action to vary the movement. For example, can they perform their action by moving high, by moving low, by travelling forwards and backwards, by moving in slow motion, by moving fast, by making it stronger, by making it lighter, by repeating part of the action several times? Let the children try all or some of these variations.

Talk to the children about the different actions involved when working with wood. Ask each member of the class to choose one of the following actions: sawing, chopping, sanding, chiselling or planing. Tell them to mime the action and then make it bigger, add a turn and change levels. Can they repeat the action three times to build up a rhythmic phrase that has a clear beginning, middle and an end? Ask the children to perform their rhythmic phrases several times to enable them to remember and repeat their movements.

Dance idea
Ask the children to work in groups of three or four. Tell them to perform their individual working actions three times together to create a group dance. Encourage them to think about their group shapes. How do they start? Can they work at different levels? Does the group move together or one at a time or one followed by the other? Give the groups time to discuss and practise their

---

Action words

| chopping | sawing | planing | chiselling | modelling | sculpting |
| drilling | hammering | building | sanding | polishing | painting |

dances. Make sure each group has a starting place and position, and then give each group a number. Tell group one to move first, followed by group two and so on until the whole class are moving. One by one, as the groups finish their working actions, ask them to remain very still, in their last position until every group in the class has finished. As an accompaniment to the dance, the children could use wooden percussion instruments to create working rhythms or they could make a tape recording of the sounds of chopping, sawing, sanding and so on to create a busy background of varying rhythms for their class dance.

Learning outcomes

In this lesson the children are involved in the interrelated processes of composing, performing and appreciating. These are the learning outcomes of this lesson and form the basis of assessment criteria linking into the Programme of Study (Common and General Requirements) and Programme of Study (Dance) in the National Curriculum.

Composing
• Explore, invent, select and refine dance movements.
• Shape a simple dance.

Performing
• Link body actions.
• Show a range of dynamics.
• Use different directions.
• Make changes of level.
• Work with a partner.
• Perform and repeat simple dance phrases.

Appreciating
• Show sensitivity when appraising others.

Follow-up ideas

The above idea could take several sessions to complete depending on the experience of the children. The woodworking actions could be developed further in different ways. Let the children try to do a working action together in pairs; for example sawing wood. Ask them to face each other and perform the action together, moving forwards and backwards. In groups, the children could choose to all do the same work action instead of individual actions. The theme could be developed by describing in movement the process of turning wood into paper; taking wood from the forest, with the working actions of the lumberjacks, floating the logs down river to the sawmill, transporting the wood to the paper mill or the factory. Any working actions from everyday activities could be chosen to develop into dance, such as washing, brushing hair or cleaning shoes, to activities such as spring-cleaning, washing the car, making the bed, shopping and so on.

3. Paper

Age range
Nine to eleven.

Movement content
What – Whole body actions, turning.
How – Quick and slow.
Where – Levels and patterns, in the air.
With whom – Small groups.

Group size
In groups of three.

What you need
Chosen stimuli: object, e.g., a large piece of paper such as a sheet of newspaper, and music, e.g., 'Orinoco flow' on *Watermark* by Enya (Warners); tape recorder.

What to do
Introduction
Ask the children to stretch into different individual body shapes; for example a narrow shape, a wide shape, a curved shape or a twisted shape. Encourage them to stretch their whole bodies from their fingertips to their toes. Tell them to stretch into these different shapes standing on two feet, on one foot, lying on their backs and on their stomachs.

Movement development
Show the class a large piece of paper. Scrunch it up, flatten it out and then scrunch it up again. Now ask the children to make their bodies into scrunched up shapes and then slowly stretch out into flat shapes. Using the words 'scrunch' and 'stretch', ask the children to make up a movement sequence. Ensure that each time they stretch they make different shapes using different levels.

Show the class the paper again and this time scrunch it up, throw it, and let it fall and land. Ask the children if they can scrunch, jump, land and stretch. Tell them to join the

movements together to form a dance motif. It is important here to talk to the class about safety and looking after their bodies when they are jumping and landing, remembering to control their bodies and being aware of other people in the class. Ask the children to repeat their dance motifs several times so that they can practise and perform the movements to ensure quality and clarity.

Ask the class to find different ways of turning; on two feet, on one foot, on their bottoms, stomachs, turning high, turning low, turning fast, turning slow and spiralling. Now tell them to select one way of turning and see if they can add it to their dance motifs so that they can scrunch, jump, land, turn and stretch.

Dance idea
Ask the children to get into groups of three; one as 'A', one 'B', and one 'C'. Now ask the group to start in a stretched out shape one at a high level, one medium and one low. A performs her motif (scrunch, jump, land, turn and stretch) then B performs his motif and joins A. Finally, C performs her motif and joins A and B. Then A, B and C scrunch up together in order to repeat this idea, but with B commencing and with C commencing the third time. Ask the trios to think about their group shapes at the beginning, when they will meet and how they will finish.

Play the music to the class and explain that the music is

Action words

stacking	piling	falling	floating	spiralling	sinking
filing	printing	folding	tearing	ripping	scrunching
smoothing	creasing	wrapping	writing	rolling	throwing

ongoing and will help their dances to flow and be continuous. Let the groups try their dances to the music several times before letting them share their dances with the rest of the class. Encourage the audience to look at the changing body and group shapes and how they work together.

Learning outcomes

In this lesson the children are involved in the interrelated processes of composing, performing and appreciating. These are the learning outcomes of this lesson and form the basis of assessment criteria linking into the Programme of Study (Common and General Requirements) and Programme of Study (Dance) in the National Curriculum.

Composing
• Explore, invent, select and refine dance movements.
• Shape a simple dance with a clear structure.

Performing
• Link body actions.
• Use narrow, wide, curled, twisted body shapes.
• Make changes of level.
• Work in small groups.
• Perform and repeat simple dance phrases.

Appreciating
• Use appropriate vocabulary to describe dance.
• Appreciate in simple terms the aesthetic quality of dance
• Show sensitivity when appraising others.

Follow-up ideas

This dance idea might take several sessions to complete in order to achieve clarity and quality of movement. It is important that the children perfect their movements and are able to see and appreciate their work and that of others because, unlike a painting or a piece of creative writing, there is no way of keeping or remembering the dance, unless photographs are taken or a video is made and this is

not always possible. This is, however, a very good method of recording dance, to enable the children to observe themselves and each other on film. Make a recording or take photographs at the beginning of the unit of work, for example in week one, and then again in week three and at the end of the unit. This will allow both pupils and teacher to observe progression through the dance idea. The finished video or photographs can be used as a record of the children's work and for assessment. Do not overuse video or photography and only record one or two dance ideas for each age range.

The topic of 'Paper' can be used in many ways for dance. For example, the paper can become an object. A newspaper could be rolled up and become a walking stick, a telescope, a baton or a baseball bat and so on. These objects could then become the stimulus for dance; the walking stick could be a prop for a Charlie Chaplin dance or the telescope may be a starting point for looking at the shapes and patterns of the stars in the galaxy. Alternatively, held opened-out, the same newspaper might become a toreador's cape and be used in a Spanish dance.

Ideas could also be taken from the content of the newspaper itself; for example combinations and shapes of letters, words or names, or a photograph coming to life. The idea of writing could also be explored; for example, ask the children each to write their name or a word using one of their feet, or their noses or one of their elbows. Then tell them to rub it out, scrunch up the paper and throw it away and then start all over again.

CHAPTER 15

Stories

This chapter considers how some of the ideas contained in a story can be extracted and used to stimulate a dance lesson. The chapter links particularly to English and reinforces the subject-based approach through which many schools are now delivering some aspects of the National Curriculum.

The long-established and ever-popular classic story The Wind in the Willows, written by Kenneth Grahame, has been selected as the stimulus for each lesson in this chapter. In their 1993 proposals the National Curriculum Council sought: 'to ensure that pupils read widely and with enjoyment, that they develop critical faculties and are introduced to those writers and texts which are of central importance to our literary heritage...' English for Ages 5 to 16 (1993). While the identification of certain aspects of a story and being able to comment upon them, the prediction of what might happen next and the expression of personal preferences, skills pertinent to dance, are mentioned at both Key Stages 1 and 2 in the English documents.

The three dance ideas which have been inspired by The Wind in the Willows are 'In the Wild Wood', 'Spring-cleaning' and 'The life cycle of a toad'.

The lesson for five- to seven-year-olds, 'In the Wild Wood', considers being in a wood and how exploring can be exciting. The lesson includes expressing changes in mood (from happy to fearful) and making tree-like body shapes. Cross-curricular links with this lesson may include looking at how long it takes for a tree to grow and how the age of a tree can be found from the rings shown in a cross-section and, in art, making bark rubbings. Talking about forests, particularly the rainforests, would link in with both science and geography. You might also like to encourage the children to find out how trees are used for paper-making. (See also the lesson on 'Paper' in Chapter 14, 'Materials', on page 145.)

The lesson for the seven- to nine-year-olds, 'Spring cleaning', uses everyday working actions and suggests how they can be abstracted through changes in size. This lesson could also link into a topic on the seasons. (See Chapter 6, 'Spring', on pages 67–76, for consideration of how our activities can be influenced by the cycle of seasons.)

The lesson for the nine- to eleven-year-olds, 'The life cycle of a toad', uses ideas of changes of size and shape for both individual and group dances. The dance idea uses the image of a large jellified mass of toad's spawn, represented by the children's individual rounded body shapes which then join together for the group shape. The main cross-curricular links are through life cycles to science and any topic that is linked with change. This is particularly relevant to history at Key Stage 1. (See also Chapter 16, 'Time and change', on pages 159–166, where this topic is considered further.)

ACTIVITIES

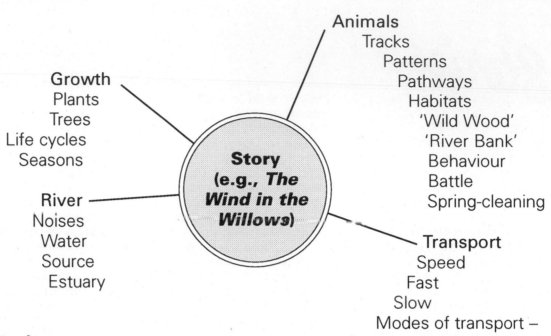

Growth
Plants
Trees
Life cycles
Seasons

River
Noises
Water
Source
Estuary

Story
(e.g., *The Wind in the Willows*)

Animals
Tracks
Patterns
Pathways
Habitats
'Wild Wood'
'River Bank'
Behaviour
Battle
Spring-cleaning

Transport
Speed
Fast
Slow
Modes of transport –
boats, cars, caravans

1. In the Wild Wood

Age range
Five to seven.

Movement content
What – Whole body actions and body shapes.
How – Quick and slow.
Where – Personal and general space.
With whom – Individuals.

Group size
Individuals.

What you need
Chosen stimulus: literature, e.g., abridged extract from Chapter 3, 'The Wild Wood' from *The Wind in the Willows* by Kenneth Grahame (page 150), and music, e.g., 'Xanadu' from *Exit Stage Left* by Rush (Mercury); tape recorder.

What to do
Introduction
Ask the children each to stand in a space, on their own and right away from anyone else. Then ask them to look at another space in the room and to run quickly to that space and then stop. Repeat this idea several times so that they are running and stopping, and then running again and stopping. Remind them to look for a space first so that they don't bump into anyone and tell them when to stop, to ensure that the amount of time spent running is quite short.

Now ask the children to skip around the room, lifting first one foot and then the other. Encourage them to weave around each other as they skip lightly around the room. Now ask them to creep quietly on tiptoe so that no one can hear them, as if they are trying to creep away. Remind them that they must be really quiet, but that sometimes they might creep quickly with small steps, if they think that they are safe, and sometimes they might creep slowly – but if they make a noise they will be caught out.

Movement development
Ask the children to space themselves out around the room and, on the spot, make tall, thin shapes or small, rounded shapes. Then ask them to change over, so that if

they are making the tall, thin shape, they should now make a small, rounded shape and vice versa. Now ask them to show you a twisted shape. Can they make their arms, their legs and their whole bodies twisted? Encourage the children to explore creating different twisted shapes and ask them to select their favourite twisted shape to show you.

Divide the class in half and call one half 'As' and the other half 'Bs'. Ask all the As to make the twisted shapes that they have selected and hold them very still. Meanwhile, tell the Bs that they are to creep slowly towards one of the twisted shapes and see if they can hide behind it. Encourage each child to find a different shape to hide behind. As soon as they have all hidden, tell the Bs to run into spaces of their own to make their twisted shapes which they should hold very still while the As then creep up and hide behind them.

Dance idea

Read the extract from 'The Wild Wood' from the Willows, on the children them how the from the happ excitement of g adventure into the wo being fearful as Mole imagines he sees faces, hears the pattering and, finally, hides away. Play the children the suggested music and ask them to listen carefully to it. Do they think music sounds creepy and rather frightening?

Start the dance idea with the children skipping around the room, as if they are quite happy to be going on an adventure. Encourage them to stop sometimes and make small, rounded shapes or tall, thin shapes as if they are playing 'Hide-and-seek', before continuing to skip. Then ask the whole class to stop and

Action words					
creeping	imagining	stumbling	chasing	crouching	looking
tiptoeing	tripping	scurrying	panting	searching	skipping
falling	pattering	trembling	investigating	treading	staring
chasing	exciting	running	hunting	hiding	fearful

There was nothing to alarm him at first entry. Twigs crackled under his feet, logs tripped him. Fungi on stumps resembled faces, and startled him for a moment. But it was all fun and exciting.

He went on to where the light was less. The trees crouched nearer and nearer, and holes made ugly mouths at him on either side. Everything was very still now. Dusk advanced on him steadily.

Then the faces began.

It was over his shoulder that he first thought he saw a face. A little evil wedge-shaped face, looking out at him from a hole. When he turned and confronted it, the thing had vanished.

He quickened his pace, telling himself not to begin imagining things. He passed another hole, and another and then—yes!—no!—yes! Certainly a little narrow face with hard eyes had flashed up for an instant from a hole and was gone.

Then suddenly, every hole, far and near, seemed to possess its face. All hard-eyed, evil and sharp.

If only he could get away from the holes in the banks, he thought, there would be no more faces. He swung off the path and plunged into the untrodden places of the wood.

Then the pattering began.

He thought it was only falling leaves at first. Then the sound grew and he knew it was the pat-pat-pat of little feet. Was it in front or behind? It seemed to be first one, and then the other, then both.

As he stood to hearken, a rabbit came running hard towards him through the trees. 'Get out of this, you fool, get out!' the Mole heard him mutter as he disappeared down a burrow.

The pattering increased till it sounded like hail on the ground. The whole wood seemed running now, hunting, chasing, closing round something—or somebody? In panic he began to run too, he knew not whither. At last he took refuge in the deep dark hollow of an old beech tree. He was too tired to run any further. He snuggled down into the dry leaves which had drifted into the hollow and hoped he was safe for a time.

He lay there panting and trembling. Now he knew that dread thing which other little dwellers in field and hedgerow had encountered here. The Rat had vainly tried to shield him from it—the Terror of the Wild Wood!

listen as you play the music; their mood should change in response to the music so that they begin to appear frightened. Can they run and stop, and run and stop, as they did at the beginning of the lesson? Then tell all the As to make their twisted shapes (to represent twisted and gnarled tree shapes), while the Bs creep around to try to hide behind them. The Bs should then run and make twisted tree shapes while the As creep around and hide behind the twisted shapes made by the Bs. The dance could end with the whole class running and stopping repeatedly, in panic, and finish with each child in a crouching shape, trembling.

When the children return to the classroom, discuss with them how the mood changed during their dance and how that was shown in their movements. At the beginning of the dance they were skipping – how do they feel when they are skipping or how do they think other children might feel if they saw them skipping? Draw out from them how their movements changed; to running and stopping to show panic and fear and, eventually, hiding. Ask them to describe the part of the dance they liked the best and to say why.

Learning outcomes
In this lesson the children are involved in the interrelated processes of composing, performing and appreciating. These are the learning outcomes of this lesson and form the basis of assessment criteria linking into the Programme of Study (Common and General Requirements) and Programme of Study (Dance) in the National Curriculum.

Composing
• Invent, select and adapt a simple phrase.
• Create movements to show moods and feelings.
• Experience a range of stimuli (stories and music).

Performing
• Contrast between movement and stillness.
• Contrast between large and small shapes.
• Move high and low.
• Work without interfering with others.

Appreciating
• Express personal preferences.

Follow-up ideas
The whole idea of being in the wood could be developed further so that a particular part of the dance space is identified as the wood and the twisted tree shapes are made in that area only for the other children to creep around and then run and hide among. The twisted tree shapes could move steadily closer together, creating the impression that the forest becomes denser the further in one travels. The running and hiding could be performed several times to extend the dance and the children could explore hiding in different ways (such as under, behind or inside), depending on the twisted tree shapes. Also, the tree shapes could be made and explored using different levels.

Action words

dusting	vacuuming	scrubbing	polishing	cleaning	brushing
washing	sweeping	decorating	wiping	whitewashing	wallpapering
painting	scraping	sparkling	drying	shaking	cutting

2. Spring-cleaning

Age range
Seven to nine.

Movement content
What – Whole body actions.
How – Quick and slow.
Where – Personal and general space.
With whom – Individuals.

Group size
Individuals.

What you need
Chosen stimuli: music (to work to), e.g., *Peter and the Wolf* by S. Prokofiev, and literature, e.g., extract from Chapter 1, 'The river bank' from *Wind in the Willows* by Kenneth Grahame (page 153); tape recorder.

What to do
Introduction
Ask the children to move about the room, weaving in and out of each other. Remind them to use all of the space and not to go too near to anyone else. Tell them to repeat this weaving in and out and, as they go, ask them to introduce a turn and then continue weaving and turning as they travel. Encourage them to turn in different ways so that sometimes they turn high and sometimes they turn low, near the floor. Their turns could be either quick or slow. Ask them to make up a phrase combining weaving, turning and stopping.

Movement development
Ask the children to gather around you and to listen carefully while you read the extract, given opposite, from 'The river bank' from *The Wind in the Willows*.

Discuss with them the various spring-cleaning activities that are mentioned in the extract and ask them each to select any action that they might do if they were spring-cleaning their houses; for example washing the windows, polishing, vacuuming, dusting, painting, and so on. Ask them to find spaces and perform their actions; making it very clear how they start and how they finish them. Tell the children each to repeat their action three times. Now ask them to perform their action once, but this time make it so big that it fills the room. Encourage them to travel all over the room and to make their actions really large. If their actions require them to reach high, then the children might even include a jump. Can they include a turn too, as they did at the beginning of the lesson? In contrast, now ask them to make their selected actions as small as they can. They will be working on the spot and in their own spaces.

Dance idea

Ask the children to think about the spring-cleaning actions that they selected and to then think about how just one part of their action might be enlarged or exaggerated. Encourage them to explore which might be the best part of their action to develop in this way and to try out ideas several times using different ways of travelling, jumping and turning to help them to enlarge this part of the action. Now ask them to think about a different part of their original action that they can make smaller. Again encourage them to try out different ideas before selecting their final way of reducing the action. Their action should now look very different from how they performed it originally, as one part of it will be exaggerated and another part will be very small. The rest of the action, though, can be performed as normal. Ask the children to repeat their new action sequence three times, so that the beginning of the next action follows on from the end of the previous action to make the whole dance continuous and flowing.

The Mole had been working very hard all the morning, spring-cleaning his little home. First with brooms, then with dusters; then on ladders and steps and chairs, with a brush and a pail of whitewash; till he had dust in his throat and eyes, and splashes of whitewash all over his black fur, and an aching back and weary arms. Spring was moving in the air above and in the earth below and around him, penetrating even his dark and lowly house with its spirit of divine discontent and longing. It was small wonder, then, that he suddenly flung down his brush on the floor, said 'Bother!' and 'O blow!' and also 'Hang spring-cleaning!' and bolted out of the house without even waiting to put on his coat.

Ask each child to find a partner with whom to sit. Let them decide in their pairs who will dance first while the other person observes. They will then change over. The person performing will need to show their original action first and then demonstrate how that action has been developed by exaggerating one part, by making one part smaller and by repeating these movements three times to create a flowing dance phrase. The person watching needs to observe carefully to see if they can identify these developments and then comment on their observations. Then let the children change over so that they each have a chance to perform and to observe.

Learning outcomes
In this lesson the children are involved in the interrelated processes of composing, performing and appreciating.

These are the learning outcomes of this lesson and form the basis of assessment criteria linking into the Programme of Study (Common and General Requirements) and Programme of Study (Dance) in the National Curriculum.

Composing
• Explore, invent, select and refine dance movements.
• Shape a simple dance with a clear structure.
• Respond to a range of stimuli: music and stories.

Performing
• Link body actions.
• Make changes of level.
• Perform and repeat simple dance phrases.

Appreciating
• Use appropriate vocabulary to describe dance.
• Show sensitivity when appraising others.

Follow-up ideas
A similar idea could be explored by the children changing the speed within their original spring-cleaning actions, so that one part of each action becomes very fast and another part becomes very slow and is performed in slow motion. Working in this way – taking an initial idea and then developing it by using changes of speed, size, level and direction – is a well-known choreographic technique.

3. Life cycle of a toad

Age range
Nine to eleven.

Movement content
What – Body shapes.
How – Quick and slow.
Where – Personal and general space.
With whom – Groups.

Group size
Groups of five.

What you need
Chosen stimulus: music, e.g., 'We all stand together' by Paul McCartney on *Rupert and the Frog Song* (MPL Communications) (video and recording); tape recorder; pens and pencils.

What to do
Introduction
Ask the children each to stand in a space on their own and then walk around the room, moving around each other using all the space. Encourage them to travel to the centre of the room and to each of the corners, to ensure that the whole space is being used. Next ask them to travel around the room, but this time starting slowly and then beginning to increase their speed. Remind them that they will need to be alert and always look for a space to move into, so that they avoid bumping into anyone else. Let them repeat this idea two or three times.

Movement development
Ask the children to get into groups of five and ask each group to sit in a space. Tell them to arrange their groups of five into line formations standing side by side, and to identify who will be the leader in each group. Each leader should then squeeze the hand of the child standing next to him or her, who in turn squeezes the hand of the next child and so on, so that a 'signal' is passed along each line. When the end of the line

Action words					
moving	stretching	splitting	disintegrating	pulsating	weaving
breaking	melting	enlarging	twisting	exploding	forming
expanding	turning	joining	darting	growing	gelling

is reached the 'signal' should be passed back. Encourage the groups to change who is the leader and to develop their own signals, for example, to a nod of the head or shaking an arm.

Now ask the children to move away from the other members of their group, so that they are in spaces on their own again. Ask them to swing their arms from side to side around their bodies so that their arms curve and wrap around their bodies. Now ask the children to move from low to high at the same time as their arms are curving around their bodies. Can they think of other ways of moving on the spot, but maintaining a rounded shape? For example they could start in a small, rounded shape. Encourage them to explore different ways of doing this, thinking about different directions and levels. Finally, ask the children each to choose one curved body action that moves from small to large and ask them to perform this idea slowly.

Dance idea

Ask the children to return to their groups of five and, one at a time, show their curved body action to the rest of their group. Tell the group to look at each of the ideas and see how each could relate to the others of the group. Tell the children that you want their individual rounded shapes to fit together to form a large rounded mass, so it may be necessary for them to adjust their ideas or their position within the group slightly to achieve this overall shape. Encourage each group to be quite clear about their group (mass) shape, so that they know exactly which parts of their bodies are in contact with another member of the group.

Ask the children to start on their own, away from each other, and then all together begin moving gradually making their individual body shapes bigger and finally forming their large, rounded, mass shapes in their groups. Once each group has formed their mass shape they need to select a leader. The leader initiates a pulsating movement which can be passed from one child to the next, until the whole group is moving together. Remind the group about when, earlier in the lesson, they were in a line and passing a 'signal' along. The

groups will need to decide in which order the pulsating signal will pass around so that everyone knows exactly when it is their turn to move. When each group has decided on the order for the signal, let them try forming their mass shape and then making the group shape pulsate. Tell them that once the whole group is moving these movements should get bigger and bigger until the group mass is forced to break up.

Discuss with the children the imagery of a jellied mass of toads' or frogs' spawn and how all the tadpoles wriggle their way out and become independent, swimming freely. Let the children listen to the suggested music and, while the music is playing, ask them to imagine the movements in their minds. Then play the music again and ask the children to take up their starting positions, on their own but near the rest of their group. When the music starts the children should all begin to move together, starting small and slowly making their body shapes larger and eventually forming the group mass. They should then begin the pulsating and pass this movement around the group until the movement is so great that the mass is forced to break up. Ask the children to think about how their group will break up. Will it be all at once or one at a time? When the group has separated, ask the children to quickly dart and weave in and out of each other, just as they did at the beginning of the lesson. Play the music several times so that the children are able to repeat their dance idea and become more confident in their movements.

When the children return to the classroom, talk to them about how the mass formed and then how it broke up and how they then moved individually. Ask them to write about their dances using appropriate vocabulary and terminology (such as changing shape, the use of levels or varying speeds) and how they relate to the life cycle of a toad or a frog.

Learning outcomes

In this lesson the children are involved in the interrelated processes of composing, performing and appreciating. These are the learning outcomes of this lesson and form the basis of assessment criteria linking into the Programme of Study (Common and General Requirements) and Programme of Study (Dance) in the National Curriculum.

Composing
• Explore, invent, select and refine dance movements.
• Shape a simple dance with a clear structure.
• Respond to a range of stimuli: music.
• Create dances which communicate ideas.

Performing
• Link body actions.
• Use extended and contracted body shapes.
• Make changes of level.

• Work in small groups.
• Perform and repeat simple dance phrases.

Appreciating
• Use appropriate vocabulary to describe dance.

Follow-up ideas

This idea could be extended by developing the section after the mass has broken up and children are darting and weaving like the tadpoles. A step pattern, using the idea of big feet, could be developed from the adult frog/toad. The step pattern could then be copied by a partner.

CHAPTER 16

Time and change

The topic of 'Time and change' makes direct links with history in the primary curriculum. 'Pupils can also use dance as a form of expression of historical understanding derived for example from the study of artefacts, sculptures and paintings. History can also explain the origins of traditional dances, Morris dancing, Maypole ceremonies, jigs and reels as well as later and modern dance forms' National Curriculum History Working Group Interim Report (1989).

The dance-specific topic web on page 160 identifies several areas where children could be given opportunities to explore how people lived, dressed and moved in the past, do so in the present and may do in the future.

Infant children often have no real concept of the past, but they can begin to understand the concept of time by thinking about their own lives and what they can remember. The lesson for five- to seven-year-olds, 'Early in the morning', uses the idea of waking up and starting the day. Everyday actions, such as washing and dressing, are explored and developed. In the classroom the children could look at graphs of what time they get up, the amount of time they spend asleep and so on. Encourage them to keep diaries and write about one week in their lives. Recording special days or events can help children to remember things in their past too. The concept of time and change can be further developed by considering different stages in human development, from babyhood to old age.

The lesson for seven- to nine-year-olds focuses on a particular period in history: Tudor and Stuart times. The children experience the way movement might have been affected by the clothing worn and learn basic period dance steps. These steps are then used as a basis for creating dances, in the style of the period, concentrating particularly on floor patterns. The use of a video is suggested to support this type of lesson to show the houses, furniture, costume and musical instruments of the period. Remember to impress upon the children that such videos are not contemporary, but modern representations.

The children can develop the whole period theme further by investigating mazes and knot gardens and how their pattterns might influence the patterns in their dances, by composing and playing their own musical scores using traditional instruments, and by investigating the designs of clothes, miniatures and jewellery.

This approach can be applied to any of the historical periods specified in the National Curriculum.

The lesson for nine- to eleven-year-olds looks at the Victorian era and contrasts street games today with Victorian games. Many cross-curricular links can be made by comparing home and school life at present with Victorian times; for example, working children, including stories such as The Water Babies by Charles Kingsley.

There are also possible links with both geography and art through looking at any local Victorian architecture.

ACTIVITIES

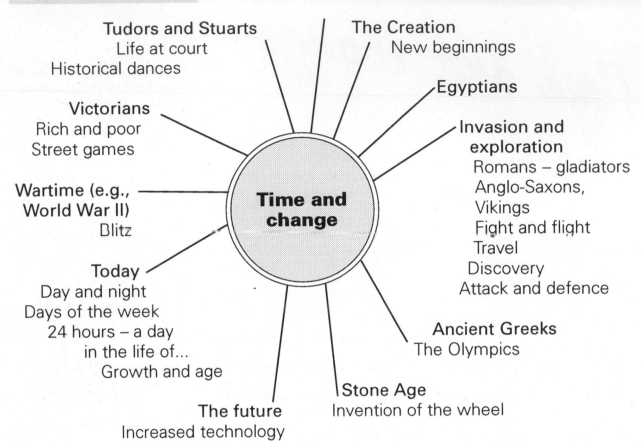

Dinosaurs

Tudors and Stuarts
Life at court
Historical dances

The Creation
New beginnings

Egyptians

Victorians
Rich and poor
Street games

Invasion and
exploration
Romans – gladiators
Anglo-Saxons,
Vikings
Fight and flight
Travel
Discovery
Attack and defence

Wartime (e.g.,
World War II)
Blitz

**Time and
change**

Today
Day and night
Days of the week
24 hours – a day
in the life of...
Growth and age

Ancient Greeks
The Olympics

The future
Increased technology

Stone Age
Invention of the wheel

1. Early in the morning

Age range
Five to seven.

Movement content
What – Body parts and shapes.
How – Quickly.
Where – Personal and general space.
With whom – Individuals.

Group size
Individuals.

What you need
Suggested stimulus: everyday actions e.g., walking; lively rhythmic music.

What to do
Introduction
Ask the children to start by walking slowly around the room, moving around each other as they go. Repeat this idea several times, but each time ask the children to move faster so that eventually they are running; hurrying around the room as if they were late. Tell them each to stop in a space and stretch their arms as high up as they can towards the ceiling and then let their arms part and come down by their sides. Let the children repeat this stretching idea and encourage them to make the movement like a giant yawning action.

Movement development
Now ask the children to sit on the floor, well away from each other in the room and facing you. Make sure that everyone can see you and then ask them to copy you as you stretch out first one arm, then the other and then both arms together. Encourage the children to look at their hands as they stretch,

so that the whole of their upper bodies are involved in the movement. Now ask them to try lying in a curled up shape on one side and try to slowly roll so that they are lying on their other side and then to begin the stretching sequence that they did with you. Ask them to go through the stretching sequence twice. They should try to end the first time through sitting up and end the second time through, standing. Allow the children enough time to try this out, so that they are quite clear about where each sequence starts and finishes.

Dance idea
Ask the children to suggest some ideas connected with getting up in the morning, such as brushing their teeth, eating breakfast, washing, brushing their hair, dressing and so on. Ask them to try and perform doing just one of these ideas, for example brushing their teeth. At first the action will be quite mimetic, but as the dance continues the action will become more abstract (which is what dance is about rather than drama). Now tell them to decide upon just one part of their chosen action and make it really big, so that they are exaggerating this part of the action. For example, when brushing their teeth, they could take the idea of the brush moving up and down and exaggerate this by imagining that they have a giant brush and huge mouth so that their movements make them stretch really high and bend down low. When the children have all decided on their action and the part that they will exaggerate, ask them to get into twos and show their actions to their partners. The person observing can try to guess what the original idea was and then they can change over, so that they both have a chance to perform and to observe. The dance can begin with everyone pretending to be curled up asleep on the floor on their sides and keeping very still. They could perform the stretching sequence so that they end sitting up, then they could repeat their stretching sequence from sitting up to standing up. They could then

Action words					
waking	tossing	turning	stretching	yawning	rising
washing	showering	drying	brushing	dressing	choosing
deciding	playing	hurrying	eating	running	drinking

run and pretend to pick up the post that has just arrived. They could perform their enlarged actions (that they have already shown to a partner) and realise that they are late and hurry out of the house to school.

Learning outcomes

In this lesson the children are involved in the interrelated processes of composing, performing and appreciating.

These are the learning outcomes of this lesson and form the basis of assessment criteria linking into the General requirements, Programme of Study (General) and Programme of Study (Dance) in the National Curriculum.

Composing

• Invent, select and adapt a simple phrase.

Performing

• Contrast between large and small shapes.
• Copy teacher's movements.
• Use of repetition.

Appreciating

• Observe and describe using appropriate dance vocabulary.
• Show sensitivity towards others when watching dance.

Follow-up ideas

The children could choose another action that they do in the morning, but this time start slowly and then speed up or they could think about walking to school and then realising that they are late, so that they end up running.

They could also think about how they travel to school; walking, riding a bicycle, in a car or on the bus. Perhaps they meet a friend on the way to school and stop and chat and then realise that they are late for school so, again, they have to hurry.

Action words

| walking | advancing | retreating | meeting | parting | circling |
| weaving | forwards | backwards | sideways | stepping | bowing |

2. Tudors – The pavane

Age range
Seven to nine.

Movement content
What – Whole body actions, stepping.
How – Slow and light.
Where – Directions, patterns and pathways.
With whom – Small groups.

Group size
Groups of four.

What you need
Chosen stimulus: video (see below) and objects, e.g., period costumes; musical accompaniment: a pavane, e.g., *Dances of the Renaissance* by Ensemble Musica Aurea (L'Oiseau Lyré) or 'Dances from Terpsichore (1612)' by M. Preatorius on *Dance Music* (Archiv Produktion) or *Two Renaissance Dance Bands* (EMI).

What to do
Introduction
Show the children a video which demonstrates the entertainment, music, dance, musical instruments, furniture and clothes of the Tudor courts; for example, *A concert for Mary Rose, The Six Wives of Henry the Eighth, A Man For All Seasons* or *Anne of a Thousand Days*. With the children, compare the costumes of the period with clothes worn today. Using a box of costumes (borrowed from a wardrobe library or the schools museum service), let the children try on different pieces of clothing: head-dresses, hats, ruffs, stomachers, baggies, soft shoes and swords. Ask the children to consider how the costume might influence the way they can move. For example, the stiff bodices, ruffs and head-dresses will restrict movement in the upper body, while long skirts and swords will restrict the size of step and the speed of the movement.

Introduce the dance lesson by asking the children to walk slowly around the room and as they pass each other acknowledge them each with a slight nod or inclination of the head. Encourage them to lift their rib cages, keep their heads up and retain an upright posture at all times.

Movement development
Teach the class the basic steps of historical dance separately first. Make sure that everyone in the class can see you as you describe and demonstrate each step. Tell them to put their feet together, heels touching, making a V shape on the floor, and, starting with the left foot, take one step forward and bring the right foot to join the left foot. This step is called 'a single' and can be performed starting with the left or with the right foot, going forwards, backwards or sideways. Now ask the children to put their feet together again and, starting with the left foot, walk forwards with the left foot, walk forwards with the right foot, walk forwards with the left foot and bring their feet together. This step is called 'a double' and can also be performed moving forwards, backwards and sideways and also round in a circle.

Using a combination of singles and doubles, ask the children to make up a simple step pattern moving forwards, backwards or sideways. Encourage them to keep the steps small and light. Play a piece of historical dance music, such as for a pavanne, and ask the children to listen to its rhythm. Can they perform their step patterns to the music? Now review the video watched at the beginning of the lesson and observe particularly the floor patterns made by any dancers.

Dance idea

Ask each child to find a partner and then join up with another pair to make a group of four. Tell each group to plan their own pavanne-style dance using a combination of single and double steps and changing floor patterns and ensuring that it has a clear beginning, middle and end. Partners within each group need to decide where they are going to start; for example facing each other, side by side, close together or far apart, so that they can meet and part or circle around each other. Play the music in the background to help the children keep the rhythm and speed of the steps. When the groups have had sufficient time to explore, select and refine their step patterns, ask each group to perform their dance to another group. Ask the group observing to use photocopiable page 190 and make a drawing showing the floor pattern from beginning to end of all the dancers in the group. An example is shown in Figure 1.

Let them show their interpretation of the floor pattern to the group that have just performed and discuss their observations with them.

If possible, let the children perform their own choreography in full period costume.

Learning outcomes

In this lesson the children are involved in the interrelated processes of composing, performing and appreciating. These are the learning outcomes of this lesson and form the basis of assessment criteria linking into the General requirements, Programme of Study (General) and Programme of Study (Dance) in the National Curriculum.

Composing

• Explore, invent, select and refine dance movements.
• Shape a simple dance with a clear structure.
• Respond to a range of stimuli: video.

Performing

• Use different directions.
• Make patterns and pathways, on the floor.
• Work in small groups.
• Perform and repeat simple dance phrases.

Appreciating

• Use appropriate vocabulary to describe dance.
• Show different ways of recording dance.
• Show sensitivity when appraising others.

Follow-up ideas

This dance idea may take several sessions to complete. The pavanne is a stately dance and can also be performed as a processional dance moving forwards and backwards. The children could also learn other dances from the period, such as an allemande, the volta, a courante, a bransle, and compare the steps and music. The dances could then be performed in a suite as they would have been when danced at court. Music and instruction for these and other dances are produced by the Dolmetsch Historical Dance Society (Hunter's Moon, Orcheston, Salisbury, Wiltshire SP3 4RP), for example: *Dances of England and France, 1450–1600* by M. Dolmetsch (1976, Da Capo Publications) and *May I Have the Pleasure?* by B. Quirey (1993, BBC).

Figure 1

Action words

playing	skipping	hopping	galloping	jumping	running
dodging	searching	seeking	looking	touching	hiding
crouching	bowling	spinning	whizzing	whipping	throwing
leaping	chanting	racing	hunting	turning	bowling

3. The Victorians – Children's street games

Age range
Nine to eleven.

Movement content
What – Whole body actions.
How – Quickly and slowly.
Where – Levels and directions.
With whom – Small groups.

Group size
Groups of three.

What you need
Chosen stimulus: visual, e.g., pictures of Victorian children playing games in the street; photocopiable page 191.

What to do
Introduction
Ask the children to start by walking around the room, in between each other. Encourage them to travel faster, but remind them to keep alert and be ready to change direction so that they avoid bumping into anyone as they run. Ask the children to think about other ways of travelling, such as hopping, skipping or galloping, for example. Try to encourage them to still travel at a lively pace, but to show a variety of ways of moving.

Movement development
Ask the children to get into groups of three and, in each group, decide who will be 'A', 'B' and 'C'. A should then make a shape, which B can hide behind and C should then look to see where B is hiding. Make sure each member of the groups has a turn at making a shape, hiding behind the shape and searching. These ideas are used in the game of 'Hide-and-seek'.

Next suggest the children think about the game of 'Tag'. Each group will need to think about the extent of their area and who is going to start. After they have tried out their game of 'Tag', ask them to stop and tell them that they can continue with their game, but that they must think about using different body parts; so, for example, A might touch B's head, then B might touch C's foot, and C might touch A's elbow. Remind them about using different levels when selecting which body parts they will tag, as well as thinking about dodging, freezing and changing direction.

Dance idea
Now show the class any photographs or pictures that you have found of Victorian children playing games and give each group a copy of photocopiable page 191, giving a list of children's street games. Ask each group to select three games from the list to work on and underline them. (The sheet is also a useful reminder of work already started, if this dance idea is continued into a subsequent session.) For each game that they have selected, encourage the group to think about including as much

action as possible. To help them develop their game idea, they should think about contrasts in shape, speed, level and direction and that they should link the three games together in some way, so that one game leads naturally into the next game and a short phrase, that can be repeated, is created. The group will also need to think about how their games will start and finish.

When the children have had a chance to try out their ideas, ask each group to find another group of three. Let them decide which group will perform their dance first while the other group observes. The groups watching should try to identify the three games selected from the photocopiable sheet and be encouraged to comment upon how the games were linked. Make sure the groups have time to change over so that everyone has an opportunity to perform and to observe.

Back in the classroom, encourage the children to discuss and write about their feelings when they are playing games. There could be some investigation into how much time the children actually spend playing games, compared with the amount of time they spend watching television or playing computer games; which may raise issues concerning what is a healthy lifestyle.

Learning outcomes
In this lesson the children are involved in the interrelated processes of composing, performing and appreciating. These are the learning outcomes of this lesson and form the basis of assessment criteria linking into the Programme of Study (Common and General Requirements) and Programme of Study (Dance) in the National Curriculum.

Composing
• Explore, invent, select and refine dance movements.
• Shape a simple dance with a clear structure.
• Create dances which communicate ideas.

Performing
• Show quality of movement with a range of dynamics.
• Work in small groups.
• Perform and repeat simple dance phrases.

Appreciating
• Understand the importance of preparing the body to dance.
• Use appropriate vocabulary to describe dance.
• Show sensitivity when appraising others.

Follow-up ideas
Some of the games could be accompanied by chants; the skipping games, for example, use a whole variety of chants, such as, 'Salt, mustard, vinegar, pepper'. The children could pre-record their own chants and playground songs to accompany their dances. Each group could link their three selected games, and then use one final chant to bring together all of the groups, so that the whole class is involved together in their interpretation of this chant. The sound of a school handbell could then stop the games as the children line up to return to their (Victorian) classroom. These games could be contrasted with playground games today, so that one half of the class shows the Victorian games while the other half shows today's games. Comment about which games from the Victorian times are still popular today.

CHAPTER 17

People and places

The topic of 'People and places' in the primary curriculum makes direct links with National Curriculum Geography, Attainment Target 2 (Knowledge and understanding of places) in local, regional, national and international contexts, and Attainment Target 4 (Human geography) considering population, settlements, communications and movements.

The dance-specific topic web on page 168 identifies several areas where children can explore people and places through movement. Young children are involved only with their immediate environment and the people with whom they regularly come into contact, such as the doctor or the person who delivers their post. Invite professional people into school or take the children to visit workplaces. Some parents with interesting jobs may be willing to visit and share their skills with the children, for example a baker demonstrating how bread is made.

The lesson for five- to seven-year-olds uses the idea of 'People who help us', exploring the activities of a police officer as a starting point for dance. The children could investigate neighbourhood watch schemes and learn about crime prevention and the use of alarms. These ideas would link in well with a personal and social education programme (PSE). Older children could make simple circuits and burglar alarms in technology. A traffic count would involve maths and road safety could be emphasised by looking at the Green Cross Code in outdoor and adventurous activities.

At Key Stage 2, children begin to discover and explore people and places further afield. The lesson for seven- to nine-year-olds uses the story of The Jungle Book by Rudyard Kipling, with the hand gestures from Indian dance and the accompaniment of Indian music. We live in a multicultural society and children need to be able to recognise dance within its social, cultural and historical context.

To introduce dances from other cultures, dance companies or groups of dancers specialising in a particular style could be invited in to school to work with the children. This is by far the best way to introduce different dance forms, rather than trying to teach an area in which you have little knowledge. It is also important that children come into contact with professional dancers and see them perform.

Children can also explore and be made more aware through dance that people have individual differences and characteristics, such as being forgetful, silly, funny and so on, and experience a range of different moods, feelings and emotions, regardless of where they come from or the colour of their skin. The lesson for nine- to eleven-year-olds explores these different moods. Making children aware of characteristics encourages them to be both sensitive and responsive. This work would link particularly with the content of most PSE programmes and with character analysis in drama. The expression of moods and feelings can also be explored through art and music.

ACTIVITIES

Cultural diversity
Asian
American
African
European
Chinese
Australian –
Aborigines

People who help us locally
Police officer
Doctor
Firefighter
Postman/woman
Refuse collector

Famous people
Historians
Explorers –
Christopher
Columbus
Scientists
Artists

People and places

People in story books
Real
Imaginary

Locations
Near and far
Holidays
Hot and cold countries

Famous places
Capitals

Friends

Characters and characteristics
Moods, feelings and emotions

1. People who help us – the police officer

Age range
Five to seven.

Movement content
What – Whole body actions.
How – Quickly and slowly.
Where – Levels and general space.
With whom – Individuals.

Group size
Individuals.

What you need
Chosen stimulus: object, e.g., toy (or real) policeman's helmet; *Cops and Robbers* by J. and A. Ahlberg (1989, Little Mammoth) (optional).

What to do
Introduction
To initiate this lesson, the children could be introduced to the book *Cops and Robbers* and could then write invitations to the local police station, to invite a police officer into school to talk about the job. Alternatively, this could be a follow-up activity to develop the ideas used in the dance lesson. Remember to send thank-you letters following the visit.

Introduce the dance idea by asking the children to move around the room taking big strides, then contrast by asking them to take really small steps. Now introduce the idea of creeping. They could be creeping away from someone or creeping up to someone. Tell them to try creeping quickly and slowly. Each time they stop, ask the children to be either high or low, as if they are hiding behind something. Ask some children to demonstrate for the rest of the class.

Movement development
Repeat the idea of creeping and stopping several times so that the children are able to develop a movement phrase and know exactly how they will stop each time.

Now return to the idea of striding and ask the children to take four big strides in any direction, stop, turn and then take four big strides back again to where they started. Let them repeat this four times so that they are able to develop a movement phrase of striding, stopping and turning.

Dance idea

Ask the children to sit down around you while you show them the (toy) policeman's helmet. Discuss with them some of the activities that a police officer might do, such as walking the beat, driving a police car, catching villains, directing the traffic and so on. Remind them that all these jobs are carried out by both policemen and policewomen.

Divide the class in half and call one half of the class 'A' and the other half 'B'. Tell the As to start with their phrases of striding, stopping and turning like a policeman four times. Meanwhile all the Bs should remain still, crouching and hiding like villains. At the end of their phrases, the As should stand still on the spot and perform arm gestures as if they are directing the traffic. Meanwhile the Bs should perform the creeping and stopping phrase that they created earlier, remembering sometimes to stop high and sometimes low as if they are hiding. Now let the children invent movements for the Bs (the robbers) snatching something, a handbag for example, and the As (the police officers) spotting them. You could blow a whistle to emphasise the theft. The As should then follow the Bs as they perform their creeping and stopping phrases again with the As trying to follow, or shadow, them.

Learning outcomes

In this lesson the children are involved in the interrelated processes of composing, performing and appreciating. These are the learning outcomes of this lesson and form the basis of assessment criteria linking into the Programme of Study (Common and General Requirements) and Programme of Study (Dance) in the National Curriculum.

Composing
• Invent, select and adapt a simple phrase.

Performing
• Move high and low.
• Use of repetition.
• Work without interfering with others.
• Contrast between movement and stillness.

Appreciating
• Observe and describe using appropriate dance vocabulary.
• Show sensitivity towards others when watching dance.

Follow-up ideas

The material in this lesson will undoubtedly take more than one lesson. The section where the policeman is shadowing the robber could be developed further and music, such as *Silent Movies* (BBC Cassettes), could be introduced here to help the children phrase this part of the dance. Let the children decide if the robber is to be caught or will eventually escape.

Action words					
striding	plodding	turning	stepping	running	catching
directing	pointing	watching	looking	planning	hiding
creeping	taking	snatching	helping	guiding	prowling
robbing	climbing	caring	pursuing	arresting	escaping

2. Dawn breaking

Age range
Seven to nine.

Movement content
What – Whole body actions and body parts.
How – Quick and slow, strong and light.
Where – Personal and general space, levels and directions.
With whom – Individuals and with partners.

Group size
Individuals, and partners.

What you need
Chosen stimulus: literature, e.g., extracts from *The Jungle Book* by Rudyard Kipling (page 171); Indian sitar music; pictures and photographs of parrots, monkeys, deer and peacocks; photocopiable page 192.

What to do
Introduction
Read the description opposite, taken from *The Jungle Book*, of dawn breaking in the Indian jungle in spring, which describes the sounds and movements of the animals and birds. Discuss with the children the individual animals and birds and their 'characteristics'; for example, proud, strutting peacocks, chattering, noisy parrots, mischievous monkeys (*bandar-log*) and nimble deer. Also tell the children a little of the background to the story, about the boy Mowgli raised by the wolves and his adventures in the jungle.

Distribute copies of photocopiable page 192, and explain the pictures of hand gestures depicting the animals and birds. These are the basic hand gestures in *kathak* which is a form of Indian dance. *Kathak* takes its movements from life and stylises them, using rhythm and music. Ask the children to copy the hand gestures given on the photocopiable page. Now tell them to find partners and show their partners their gestures and let them try to guess which animal or bird is being represented.

Movement development
Ask the children to run around the room, dodging and darting to avoid bumping into anyone. Now ask them to move to this phrase, 'Walk, walk, walk, walk, run, run, run, stop'. As they perform this movement phrase, suggest that the children think about the way in which monkeys might stand and move. Photographs might help here, for the children to look at the posture of monkeys and how they use their hands and feet to walk and run. Encourage the children to think about how they might start and finish their movement phrases.

As a contrast to the movements of the monkey, ask the children to consider the movements of a peacock, moving to the phrase, 'Walk, walk, walk and stop'. Ask them to make the walking action proud and tall, extending their necks as much as possible. When they stop, tell them to try to spread their bodies into large shapes and turn slowly round in a circle, just like a peacock displaying his beautiful fan-like tail. Can the children put the two movement phrases together now – the monkey phrase and the peacock phrase? Now ask the class to think about the flight movements of parrots and the nimble stepping and leaping of deer. Allow the children adequate time to try out their ideas and encourage them to change levels and directions as they move.

Action words					
walking	strutting	spreading	flying	swooping	hovering
preening	settling	perching	running	dodging	darting
stepping	cautious	delicate	nimble	jumping	quick

As the dawn was breaking the Sambhur belled
    Once, twice and again!
And a doe leaped up and a doe leaped up
From the pond in the wood where the wild deer sup.

from 'Hunting-song of the Seeonee Pack'

They were lying out far up the side of a hill overlooking the Waingunga, and the morning mists lay below them in bands of white and green. As the sun rose they changed into bubbling seas of red and gold, churned off, and let the low rays stripe the dried grass on which Mowgli [the man-cub] and Bagheera [the black panther] were resting. It was the end of the cold weather, the leaves and the trees looked worn and faded, and there was a dry ticking rustle when the wind blew. A little leaf tap-tap-tapped furiously against a twig as a single leaf caught in a current will.

...Mowgli sat with his elbows on his knees looking out across the valley at the daylight. Somewhere down in the woods below a bird was trying over in a husky, reedy voice the first few notes of his spring song. It was no more than a shadow of the full-throated tumbling call he would be crying later, but Bagheera heard the scarlet woodpecker.

...In an Indian jungle the seasons slide one into the other almost without division. There seem to be only two – the wet and the dry, but if you look closely below the torrents of rain and the clouds of char and dust you will find all four going round in their regular order. Spring is the most wonderful, because she has not only to cover a clean bare field with new leaves and flowers, but to drive before her and to put away the hanging-on, over-surviving raffle of half-green things which the gentle winter has suffered to live, and to make the partly dressed, stale earth feel new and young once more. And this she does so well that there is no spring in the world like the Jungle spring.

...*That* is the noise of the spring – a vibrating boom which is neither bees nor falling water nor the wind in the tree-tops, but the purring of the warm, happy world.

...When the morning came, and Mor, the peacock, blazing in bronze and blue and gold, cried ... aloud all along the misty woods ... Mor cried the new smells, the other birds took it over.... There was a yelling and scattering of *bander-log* (monkeys) in the new-budding branches above ....

peacocks showing off their fan-like tails and, finally, the mischievous play of the monkeys. Play some Indian sitar music to accompany the children's performance.

Learning outcomes

In this lesson the children are involved in the interrelated processes of composing, performing and appreciating. These are the learning outcomes of this lesson and form the basis of assessment criteria linking into the Programme of Study (Common and General Requirements) and Programme of Study (Dance) in the National Curriculum.

Composing

• Explore, invent and select dance movements.
• Shape a simple dance with a clear structure.
• Respond to a range of stimuli: stories and music.

Performing

• Link body actions.
• Isolate body parts.
• Show quality of movement and dynamics.
• Use different directions.
• Make changes of level.
• Work with a partner.
• Perform and repeat simple dance phrases.

Appreciating

• Show sensitivity when appraising others.

Follow-up ideas

This lesson idea contains sufficient material for several sessions. The class could develop the dance further by working in large groups; for example, as a herd of deer, a troupe of monkeys, or a flock of parrots. This will encourage the children to think of changing group shapes.

Dance idea

Ask the children to find partners and decide on which movement phrase they would like to work – the monkey, the peacock, the parrot or the deer phrase. Using the movements that they have worked on during the lesson, tell the children to try to make up dances with their partners, ensuring that they have distinct starting positions, middles and clear finishes. Let them try out and select some ideas with their partners, for example both moving together, moving one at a time, one moving and then the other, one moving high and the other moving low, dancing side by side, one behind the other, or meeting and parting. At some point during their dances, encourage them to include the *kathak* hand gestures to symbolise the animal or bird that they have chosen.

With the whole class, now create a dance of the dawn breaking. Ask the children to take up their starting positions around the room with their partners. Let the children using parrot-like movements start, with swooping and perching, followed by the cautious deer movements, the

3. Moods, feelings and emotions

Age range
Nine to eleven

Movement content
What – Whole body actions and body shapes.
How – Quick and slow, strong and light.
Where – Levels.
With whom – Individuals, with partners and in groups.

Group size
Individuals, partners and in groups.

What you need
Chosen stimulus: words and images, e.g., words to convey moods, feelings and emotions written on to a pack of cards.

What to do
Introduction
Ask the children to stand in the middle of the room as close to each other as possible without touching. Now tell them to try to weave in between each other still keeping very close. Then ask them to walk away as far away from each other as possible, so that they are alone. Ask the class to repeat this idea several times so that they feel what it is like to be close together in a group and, in contrast, far apart and on their own. Now ask them each to walk towards someone, hold both their partner's hands, lean away from each other and, using each other's weight, sit down on the floor and stand up again. They should then walk away from this partner to meet someone else and repeat the same movements. This activity will encourage the idea of trusting and supporting each other. Talk to the class about what it feels like to be alone, to have a friend, and to be part of a group.

Movement development
Write contrasting words conveying emotions on to cards (for example, 'happy' and 'sad') and make a pack of cards using all or some of the words suggested in the 'Action words' section of this lesson plan. To use the cards, ask the children each to choose one.

Ask them to consider the first word on the card and choose a sculptured shape to convey it. Ask them to experiment and try several shapes at different levels. Now tell them to choose three of the body shapes they have devised, one near the floor, one high and one at a medium level, and join them together in any order by adding a turn, a travelling action or a jump. Can they now try the same idea with the second, contrasting word on the card and choose three body shapes, joining them together with a turn, a travelling action or a jump? Now let them try mixing the body shapes using the contrasting words; for example, the words 'happy'

Action words					
Happy	content	glad	pleased	cheerful	excited
fortunate	sad	sorrowful	distressed	shocked	angry
displeased	resentful	irritable	pained	loud	calm
tranquil	quiet	still	serene	confident	tense
strained	tight	rigid	stern	nervous	excitable
highly-strung	agitated	afraid	timid	confident	bold
trusting	lonely	alone	isolated	together	cold
in company	united	belonging	devastated	unwanted	alone

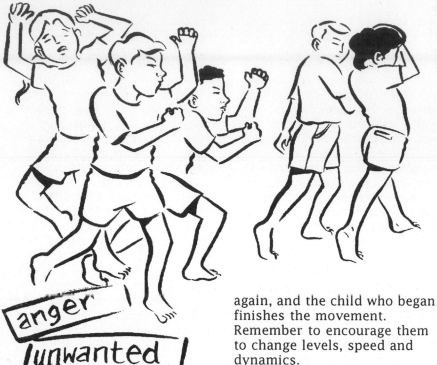

anger

unwanted

and 'sad' could be: first and second 'happy' body shapes, first 'sad' body shape, third 'happy' body shape, second and third 'sad' body shapes. Ensure the class have sufficient time to practise and refine their movements. Encourage them to think not only about their body shapes and the actions they are making to link them together, but also to consider the speed and the strength of the movements to show a contrast. Ask each child to show their ideas to a partner. Can they guess the words that their partner's were given? Ask them to continue working with their partners using all the words they have been working on individually. Tell them to choose two of the words and have a 'conversation'; for example, one partner moves and then the other partner moves, then they move together, the second child moves, they move together again, and the child who began finishes the movement. Remember to encourage them to change levels, speed and dynamics.

Dance idea
Ask the class to get into groups of six. Choose five words from the pack of cards for them to use as the starting point for their dance. For example, the words might be 'happy', 'angry', 'tense', 'friends', and 'unwanted', or 'alone', 'sad', 'resentful', 'united' and 'strong'. Encourage the groups to discuss the movements and group relationships that will convey the meanings of these words and to make sure that their dances have beginnings, middles and ends. Ask the groups to think about how they will work together; individually, one after the other, three versus three, five against one and so on. When the groups have completed their dances, ask each group to show their dance to the rest of the class and describe the words they chose and how they set about choreographing their dance. It is just as important that the children can talk about how they created their own dance, as it is for them to appreciate the work of others.

Learning outcomes
In this lesson the children are involved in the interrelated processes of composing, performing and appreciating. These are the learning outcomes of this lesson and form the basis of assessment criteria linking into the Programme of Study (Common and General Requirements) and Programme of Study (Dance) in the National Curriculum.

Composing
• Explore, invent, select and refine dance movements.
• Shape a simple dance with a clear structure.
• Create dances which communicate feelings, moods and ideas.

Performing
• Link body actions.
• Show quality of movement with a range of dynamics.
• Make changes of level.
• Work with a partner.
• Work in small groups.
• Perform and repeat simple dance phrases.

Appreciating
• Use appropriate vocabulary to describe dance.
• Show sensitivity when appraising others.

Follow-up ideas
The above dance ideas contain sufficient material to cover several sessions with almost infinite variety through the combinations of words and movement. The children could go on to choose emotion-filled words for themselves and let the audience try to guess the feelings being expressed.

PHOTOCOPIABLES

The pages in this section can be photocopied and adapted to suit your own needs and those of your class; they do not need to be declared in respect of any photocopying licence. Each photocopiable page relates to a specific dance lesson in the main body of the book and the appropriate activity and page references are given above each photocopiable sheet.

Floor patterns, page 128

• Draw your floor pattern. Indicate where you started and where you finished.

The Victorians – Children's street games, page 165

• Choose three games from the list below and underline the ones your group selected:

hopscotch

skipping

spinning a top

hide-and-seek

one potato...

...ices

...e you observed?

Balloons: 1, page 106

Photocopiable pages 183

Photocopiable pages 191

Stimuli for dance – music, page 29

Song/piece	Tape title/number	Tape counter number	Topic/useful for...

Photocopiable pages

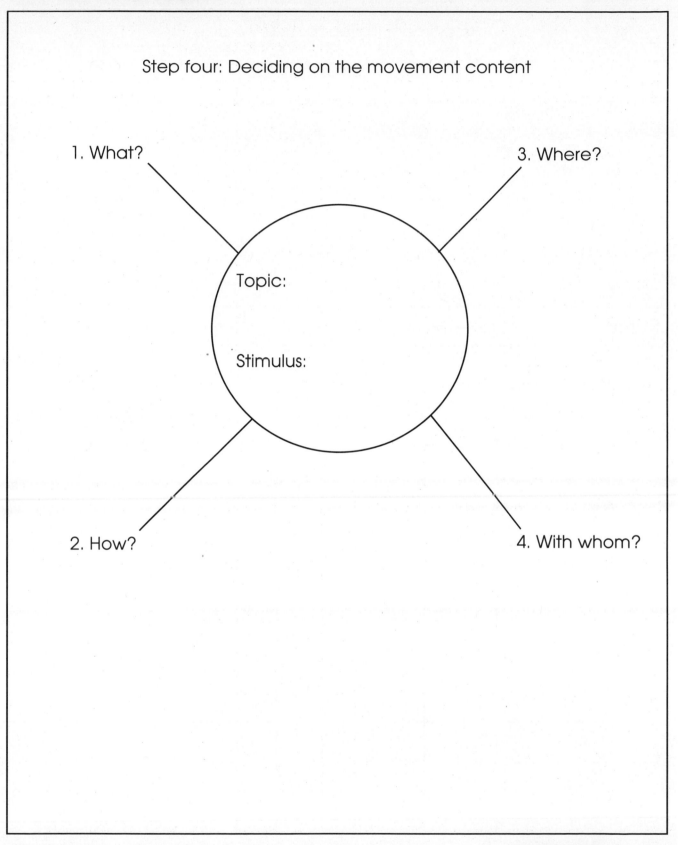

Step four: Deciding on the movement content

1. What?

3. Where?

Topic:

Stimulus:

2. How?

4. With whom?

Assessment in dance at Key Stage ☐

Year: Class:

Unit of work:

Learning Outcomes
Composing:

Performing:

Appreciating:

Name	Composing	Performing	Appreciating	Comments

Waiting at the window

These are my two drops of rain
Waiting at the window pane.

I am waiting here to see
Which the winning one will be.

Both of them have different names.
One is John and one is James.

All the best and all the worst
Comes from which of them is first.

James has just begun to ooze.
He's the one I want to lose.

John is waiting to begin.
He's the one I want to win.

James is going slowly on.
Something sort of sticks to John.

John is moving off at last.
James is going pretty fast.

John is rushing down the pane.
James is going slow again.

James has met a sort of smear.
John is getting very near.

Is he going fast enough?
(James has found a piece of fluff.)

John has hurried quickly by.
(James was talking to a fly.)

John is there, John has won!
Look! I told you! Here's the sun!

A. A. Milne

• Select one of the following patterns and draw it in the air using your forefinger or whole hand:

• Draw the pattern you chose to make on the floor in the space below:

- Look at the examples of body shapes below.

- With your partner, identify and draw a circle around each of the shapes that you observe in the partner dance that you are watching.

spread flat

long and thin

like a ball

like a screw

• Write down the three words which you chose to describe how your sea creature moved:

1 _____

2 _____

3 _____

•Now draw your fantasy sea creature below:

• Draw the four stages of enlarging your balloon shape, with the balloon getting bigger with each breath.

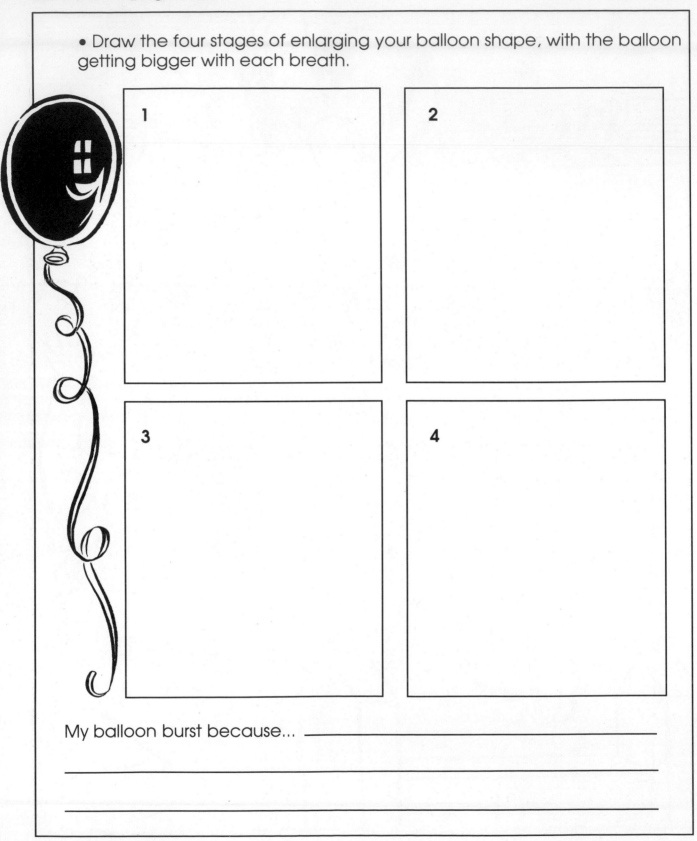

| 1 | 2 |
| 3 | 4 |

My balloon burst because... _____

_____

_____

• Look at the following trio formations:

• Try out some of these formations. Use at least two different formations in your dance.

• Can you think of any more formations? Draw them below.

• Draw a circle around the four body parts that you used while making your rhythmic dance phrase:

• Draw a picture of yourself either: under an umbrella; holding an umbrella; or, making an umbrella shape.

head

foot

ankle

shoulder

elbow

knee

arm

toe

back

hand

leg

face

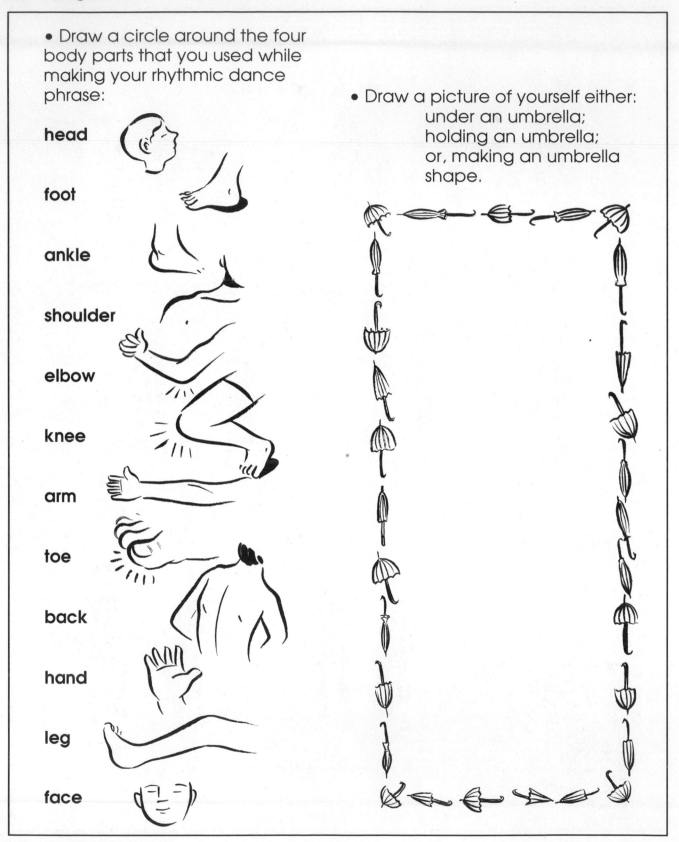

• Put a circle around the ways in which you worked with your partner.

side by side

back to back

facing each other

meeting

parting

follow-my-leader

going round

• Draw your floor pattern. Indicate where you started and where you finished.

• Draw a detailed diagram of how you imagine your group machine to look. Label all the parts and show clearly how it works.

• Complete the following:

Our machine started when... _____

_____

_____

Our machine stopped because... _____

_____

_____

• Observe the group perform their pavanne
and draw the floor patterns of all the dancers.

• Choose three games from the list below and underline
the ones your group selected:

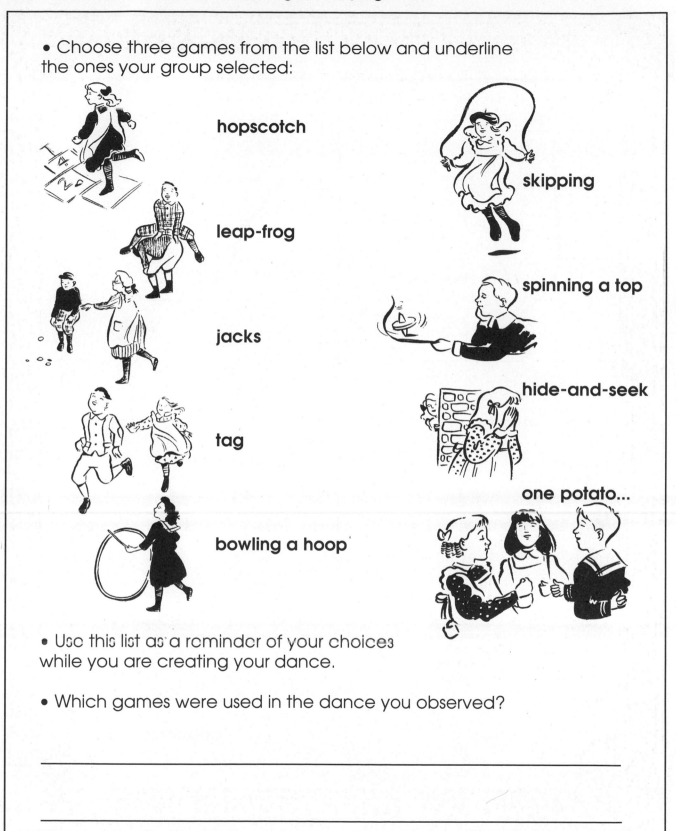

hopscotch

leap-frog

jacks

tag

bowling a hoop

skipping

spinning a top

hide-and-seek

one potato...

• Use this list as a reminder of your choices
while you are creating your dance.

• Which games were used in the dance you observed?

_____

_____

The pictures below show the basic hand gestures in *kathak* dance.

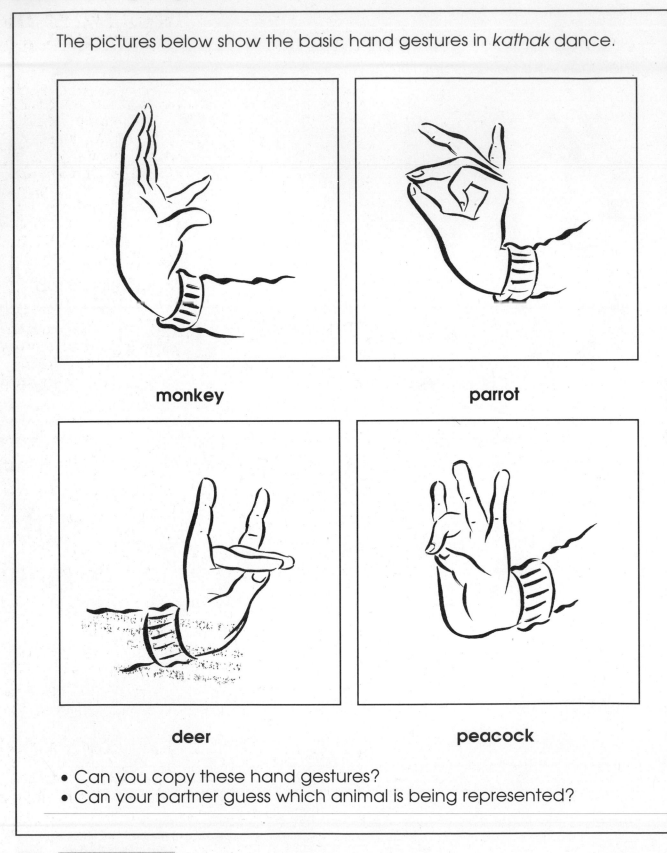

monkey

parrot

deer

peacock

- Can you copy these hand gestures?
- Can your partner guess which animal is being represented?